EASY-TO-COOK

VEGETABLES

Jacqueline Clark

BROCKHAMPTON PRESS
LONDON

First published in Great Britain in 1992 by
Anaya Publishers Ltd,
Strode House, 44–50 Osnaburgh Street, London NW1 3ND

This edition published 1996 by Brockhampton Press,
a member of Hodder Headline PLC Group

Copyright © Collins & Brown 1996

Managing Editor: Janet Illsley
Photographer: James Murphy
Designer: Pedro Prá-Lopez
Food Stylist: Jacqueline Clark
Background Artist: Annabel Playfair

All rights reserved. No part of this publication may be
reproduced, stored in a retrieval system, or transmitted,
in any form or by any means, electronic, mechanical,
photocopying, recording or otherwise, without the
permission of the copyright holder.

British Library Cataloguing in Publication Data
Clark, Jacqueline
Easy to cook vegetables. – (Easy to cook)
641.6

ISBN 1 86019 220 3

Typeset in UK by SX Composing Ltd, Rayleigh
Colour reproduction by J. Film Process, Bangkok
Printed in UK by BPC Paulton Books Ltd

NOTES

Ingredients are listed in metric and imperial measures.
Use either set of quantities but not a mixture of both.

All spoon measures are level:
1 tablespoon = one 15 ml spoon
1 teaspoon = one 5 ml spoon.

Use fresh herbs and freshly ground black pepper unless otherwise stated.

Use standard size 3 eggs unless otherwise suggested.

CONTENTS

INTRODUCTION

PAGE 5

STARTERS

PAGE 6

SOUPS

PAGE 26

MAIN COURSES

PAGE 38

ACCOMPANIMENTS

PAGE 62

SNACKS

PAGE 84

INDEX

PAGE 95

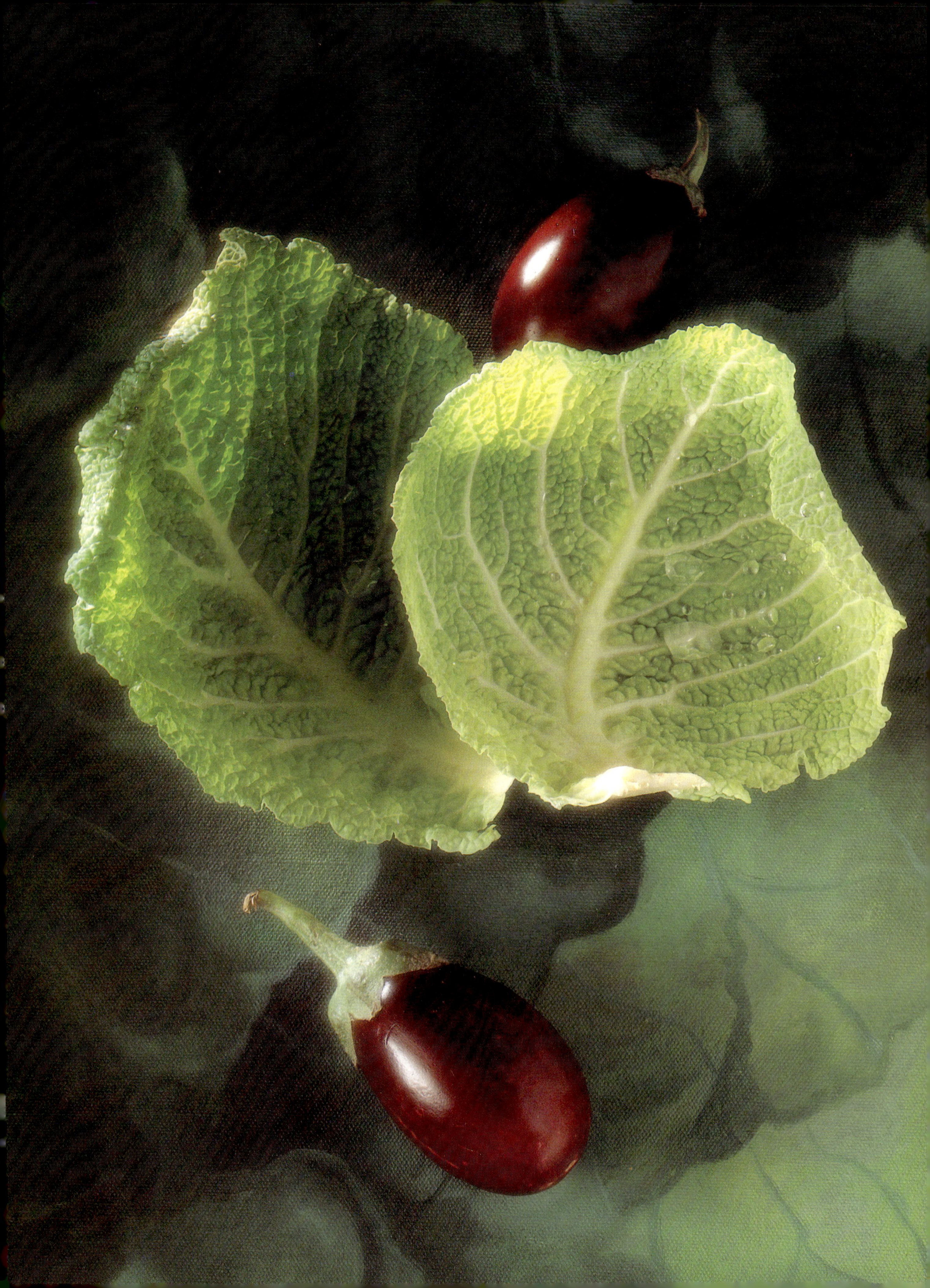

INTRODUCTION

Consider the endless variety of vegetables that fill our markets, greengrocers and supermarkets and I'm sure you will agree that they are among the most exciting foods available. Nothing can match the multitude of colours, flavours and textures of roots, shoots, leaves, bulbs, pulses and fungi on offer. Imported produce from far-flung places enables us to choose vegetables which may be out of season in this country. For example, asparagus from Chile, and courgettes from Italy or Egypt. When it comes to salad leaves we are spoilt for choice. Try the more colourful varieties available: radicchio and frilly-edged lollo rosso have distinctive flavours and look most attractive mixed with green leaves.

I'm lucky enough to live near a fruit and vegetable market – a five minute walk and I'm surrounded by tempting colourful arrays of fresh produce. Stalls specializing in West Indian varieties are piled high with sweet potatoes, yams, plantains and fiery chillies. One stall features Mediterranean vegetables – huge, shiny peppers, plum-shaped tomatoes, boxes of lamb's lettuce and rocket, sturdy bundles of asparagus and, sometimes, a tempting selection of wild mushrooms. Of course, our home-grown produce is everywhere. Neat stacks of carrots sit alongside purple-tinged turnips. Potatoes lie in earthy piles next to crinkled, leafy cabbages and dark green spinach. Varieties vary with the seasons, but a busy market is a constant source of inspiration.

Canned and frozen vegetables are useful stand-bys, particularly for quick meals and soups. Here too, the choice has widened and supermarkets now stock a good variety. Frozen mixed vegetables for stir-frying and ready chopped spinach are most useful. Canned pulses – such as haricot beans, flageolets and chick peas – save time because there's no need to soak and cook them. Canned chopped tomatoes are invaluable for soups and sauces, imparting colour and flavour.

Although the recipes in this book are not necessarily vegetarian, many of them are because with such choice and versatility meat and fish naturally play a minor role. Vegetables offer valuable minerals and vitamins; they are also a good source of dietary fibre.

Of the many different ways of cooking vegetables, steaming is by far the most successful method for retaining vitamin C. It also helps preserve colour, flavour and shape, in the case of more delicate varieties. To minimise nutrient loss, avoid boiling vegetables in a large volume of water. Other methods, such as roasting, grilling, frying and braising suit many vegetables. The possibilities are endless.

Finally, when buying vegetables, look for the healthiest specimens. Avoid any with blemishes, yellow-tinged leaves or bruises. Colours should be bright, skins smooth and firm, and generally the vegetables should look good enough to eat!

STARTERS

This is my favourite part of the meal. A starter should delight the eye as well as the tastebuds, and whet the appetite just sufficiently for the courses to follow. Alternatively you may like to compose a meal entirely of starters – the choice is up to you.

Brightly coloured baby vegetables are perfect as starters – either marinated, served as crudités, or grilled. Simple vegetables, such as mushrooms and tomatoes, can be transformed into tasty first courses by filling with imaginative stuffings. Use fresh herbs and pretty salad leaves to complete the picture.

CONTENTS

BABY CORNS WITH PEPPER SALSA	8
GRILLED VEGETABLES WITH PESTO	8
ASPARAGUS IN PROSCIUTTO	10
MARINATED BABY AUBERGINES	10
ARTICHOKE WITH GOAT'S CHEESE	12
STUFFED MUSHROOMS	12
CARROT ROULADE	14
LEEK & PEPPER SLICE	14
MUSHROOM RAGOÛT	16
TOMATO SOUFFLÉS	16
RATATOUILLE TARTLETS	18
RED ONION & OLIVE TARTLETS	18
SPICED VEGETABLES IN POPPADUM CUPS	20
CRUDITÉS WITH PEPPER DIP	20
VEGETABLE TEMPURA	22
SPICY GLASS NOODLE SALAD	22
POTATO SKINS WITH HERB DIP	24
GUACAMOLE	24

BABY CORNS WITH PEPPER SALSA

SERVES 4

If fresh baby corn cobs are not available, use canned cobs instead for this tasty colourful dish.

50 g (2 oz) butter
500 g (1 lb) baby corn cobs

SALSA
1 large red pepper, cored, seeded and chopped
1 red chilli, seeded and chopped
1 bunch spring onions, chopped
1 large beef tomato, chopped
4 tablespoons chopped coriander
¼ teaspoon salt
2 tablespoons chopped parsley
pepper to taste

TO GARNISH
coriander sprigs

1. To make the salsa, place the red pepper, chilli, spring onions, tomato, coriander, salt and parsley in a food processor or blender and work briefly to a finely chopped mixture. Season with pepper.

2. Melt the butter in a frying pan, add the baby corns and sauté for about 8 minutes until lightly golden and just tender.

3. Arrange the corn cobs on individual plates and add a spoonful of pepper salsa to each serving. Garnish with coriander.

GRILLED VEGETABLES WITH PESTO

SERVES 4

Take advantage of the smaller varieties of vegetables appearing in markets and supermarkets today – and treat them simply. This dish also makes a good accompaniment to roast lamb.

4 tablespoons olive oil
125 g (4 oz) baby courgettes
125 g (4 oz) baby corn
125 g (4 oz) button mushrooms
125 g (4 oz) cherry tomatoes
4 tablespoons pesto
basil leaves to garnish

1. Preheat grill to high. Toss the vegetables in 2 tablespoons olive oil and place in a single layer in the grill pan.

2. Place under the grill and cook for 4-6 minutes until the vegetables are slightly blackened, turning them as necessary.

3. Mix the pesto with the remaining olive oil.

4. Place the warm vegetables in a serving dish and drizzle with the pesto dressing. Garnish with basil leaves to serve.

ABOVE: BABY CORNS WITH PEPPER SALSA   BELOW: GRILLED VEGETABLES WITH PESTO

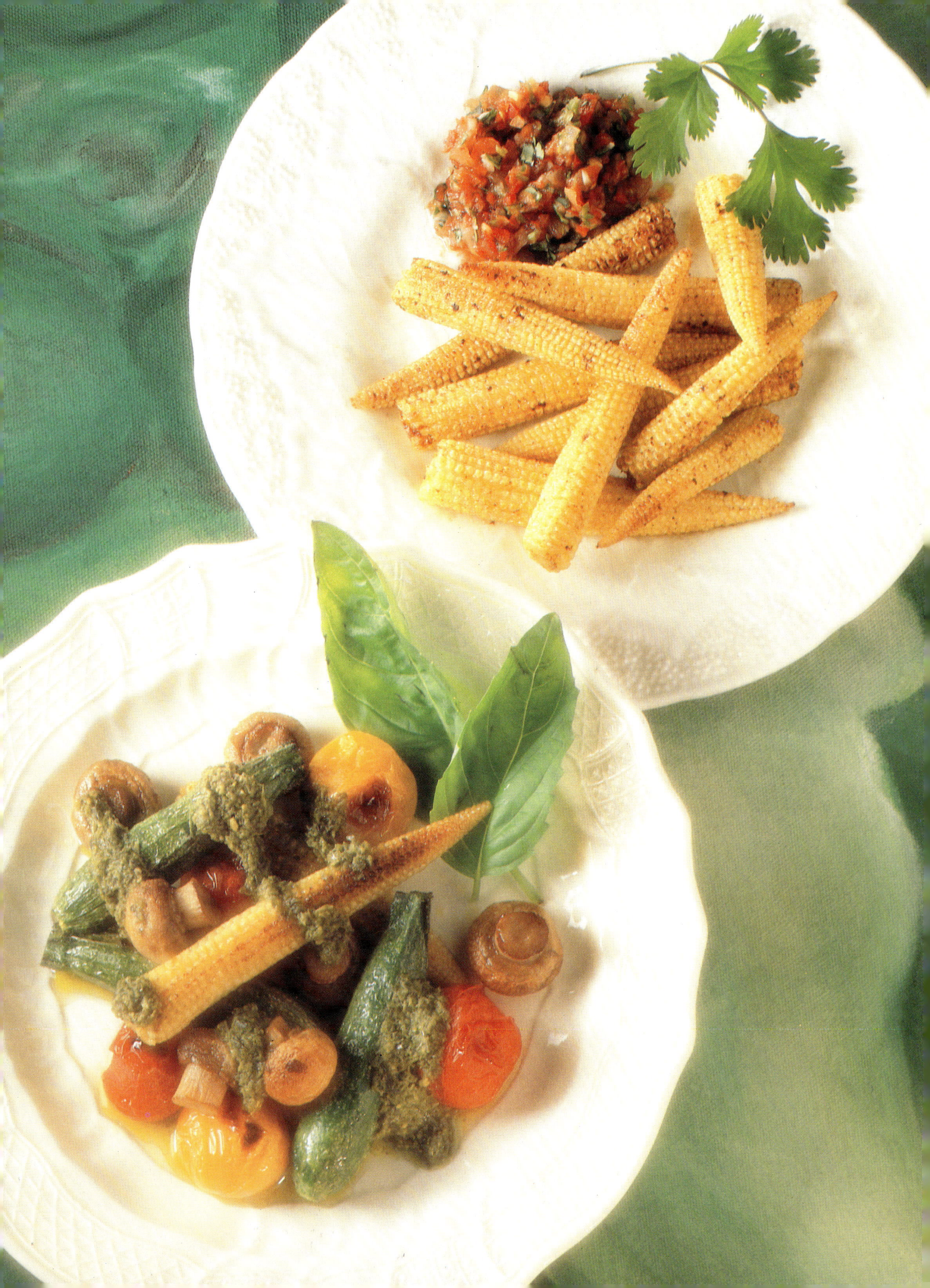

STARTERS

ASPARAGUS IN PROSCIUTTO

SERVES 4

This dish also works well served as 'finger food' for a party or buffet. Use fairly thick asparagus spears – they are easier to wrap.

12 asparagus spears, trimmed
90 ml (3 fl oz) quality olive oil
2 tablespoons white wine vinegar
1 teaspoon wholegrain mustard
salt and pepper to taste
12 thin slices prosciutto

1. Place the asparagus in a large pan of boiling salted water and cook for about 8 minutes until tender. Drain, then plunge the asparagus spears into cold water to preserve the colour.

2. Mix together the olive oil, vinegar, mustard and seasoning in a shallow dish.

3. Drain the asparagus thoroughly and toss in the olive oil mixture until well coated.

4. Carefully wrap each asparagus spear in a slice of prosciutto.

5. Arrange the asparagus spears on a serving platter and serve with crusty Italian bread.

MARINATED BABY AUBERGINES

SERVES 4

If baby aubergines are unavailable use the larger variety, cut into quarters. The flavour of this dish is even better if it is made the day before.

12 baby aubergines, halved lengthwise
225 ml (8 fl oz) quality olive oil
juice of 1 lemon
2 tablespoons red wine vinegar
3 cloves
3 tablespoons pine nuts
3 tablespoons sultanas
1 tablespoon sugar
1 bay leaf
large pinch of dried crushed chillies
salt and pepper to taste
rocket leaves to garnish

1. Preheat grill to medium high. Brush the aubergines with olive oil and place, cut side up, in the grill pan. Grill for 10 minutes, until slightly blackened, turning halfway through cooking.

2. Mix together the remaining olive oil, lemon juice, vinegar, cloves, pine nuts, sultanas, sugar, bay leaf, chillies and seasoning.

3. Place the hot aubergines in a shallow dish and pour over the marinade. Leave to cool, turning occasionally.

4. Serve cold, garnished with rocket leaves.

ABOVE: ASPARAGUS IN PROSCIUTTO *BELOW*: MARINATED BABY AUBERGINES

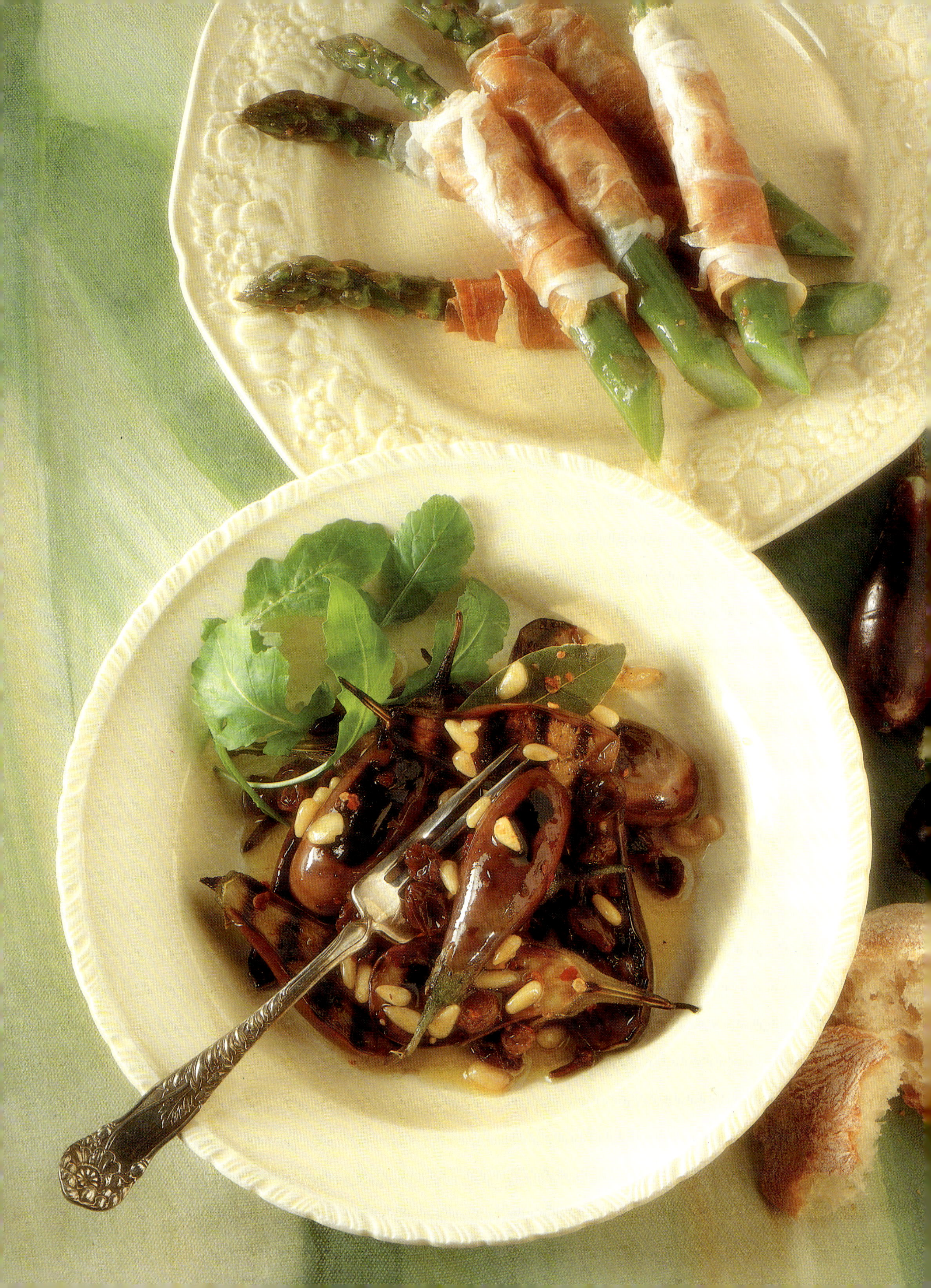

STARTERS

ARTICHOKE WITH GOAT'S CHEESE

SERVES 6

Canned artichoke bottoms make this dish a sophisticated starter that can be assembled in minutes. Look out for olive purée in good delicatessens. Alternatively, use finely chopped black olives.

2×297 g (10 oz) cans artichoke bottoms
4 tablespoons olive purée
2 crottins (small, round goat's cheese)
25 g (1 oz) flaked almonds

TO SERVE
salad leaves, eg radicchio, frisée and lamb's lettuce
olive oil for drizzling

1. Preheat grill to medium. Drain the artichoke bottoms, rinse and dry thoroughly on kitchen paper. Trim the bases if necessary to enable them to stand upright.

2. Divide the olive purée between the artichokes, spreading it into the hollows.

3. Cut the crottins into the same number of slices as there are artichoke bottoms. Place a crottin slice on each artichoke and sprinkle with almonds.

4. Grill for 5-10 minutes, until the cheese is melting and the almonds are browned.

5. Divide the salad leaves between individual serving plates. Place the artichoke bottoms on the plates and drizzle with a little olive oil. Serve immediately.

STUFFED MUSHROOMS

SERVES 4

Try using walnuts or almonds instead of the hazelnuts in this tasty filling.

12 even-sized open cup mushrooms
1 tablespoon olive oil
15 g (½ oz) butter
½ small onion, chopped
2 tablespoons chopped hazelnuts
1 clove garlic, crushed
150 g (5 oz) frozen chopped spinach, defrosted and squeezed dry
25 g (1 oz) feta cheese, crumbled
25 g (1 oz) Cheddar cheese, crumbled
1 tablespoon dried dill
salt and pepper to taste
dill sprigs and salad leaves to garnish

1. Preheat oven to 200°C (400°F/Gas 6).

2. Remove the stems from the mushrooms and chop them roughly.

3. Heat the olive oil and butter in a pan, add the onion and cook until soft. Add the chopped mushroom stems, nuts and garlic and cook for 1 minute. Add the spinach and cook for 5 minutes, stirring. Remove from the heat and stir in the cheeses and dill.

4. Arrange the mushrooms cup side up in a baking dish. Season the stuffing and divide equally between them.

5. Bake for 10 minutes or until the filling is lightly browned. Serve immediately, garnished with dill and salad leaves.

ABOVE: ARTICHOKE WITH GOAT'S CHEESE *BELOW:* STUFFED MUSHROOMS

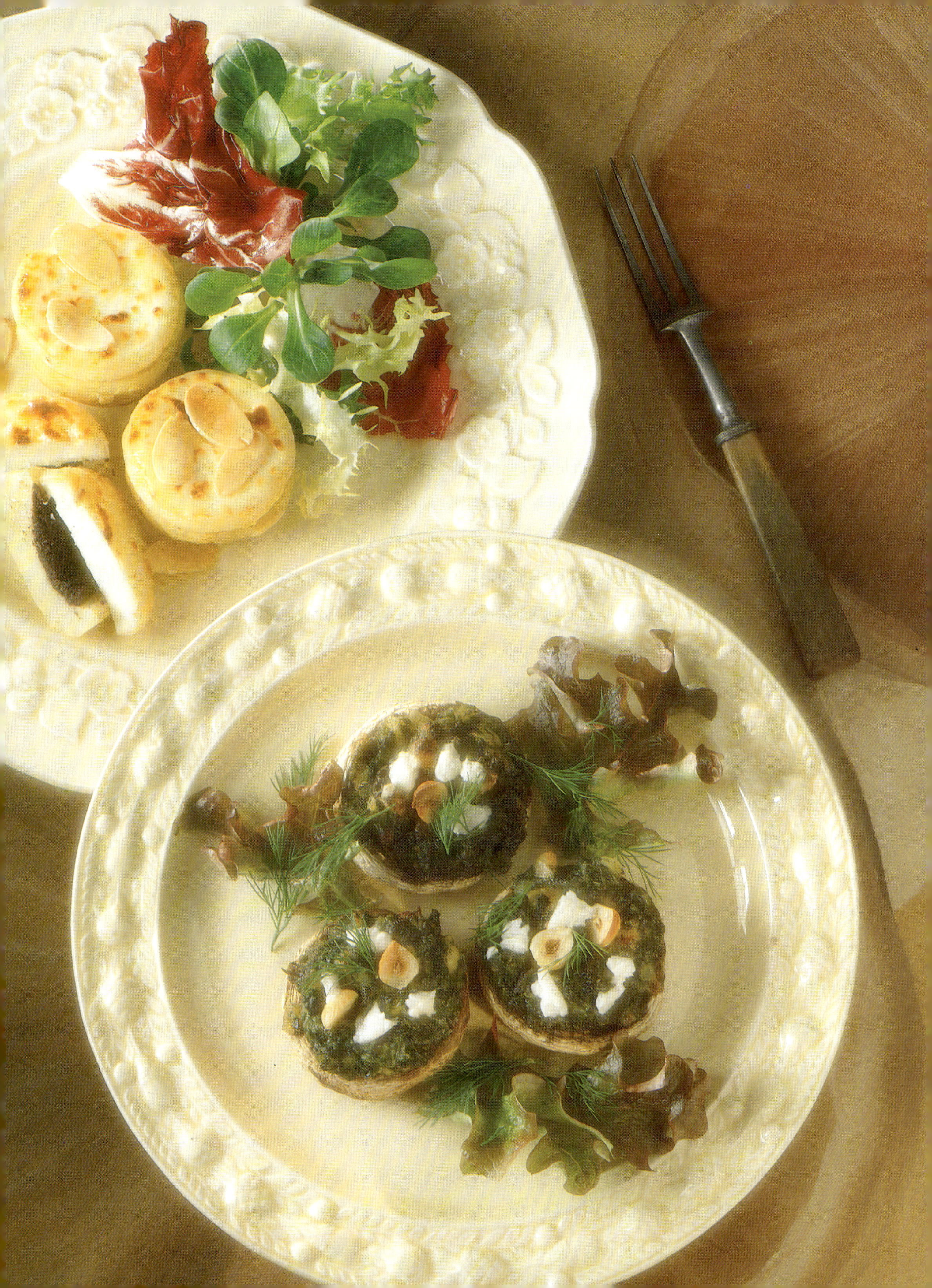

CARROT ROULADE

SERVES 6

125 g (4 oz) butter
750 g (1½ lb) carrots, finely grated
6 eggs, separated
salt and pepper to taste

FILLING
6 hard-boiled eggs, chopped
300 ml (½ pint) mayonnaise
2 tablespoons chopped chives

TO GARNISH
salad leaves

1. Preheat oven to 200°C (400°F/Gas 6).

2. Line a 34×27 cm (13½×10½ inch) Swiss roll tin with foil; brush lightly with oil.

3. Melt the butter in a pan, add the grated carrots and cook gently until soft. Transfer to a bowl and beat in the egg yolks and seasoning.

4. Whisk the egg whites until soft peaks form, then fold into the carrot mixture.

5. Spread evenly in the prepared tin and bake for 10 minutes, or until golden and springy to the touch. Cover with a clean damp cloth.

6. Mix together the ingredients for the filling and add seasoning to taste.

7. Remove cloth and turn the roulade out on to a sheet of non-stick paper. Spread with the filling, leaving a 1 cm (½ inch) border all round. Carefully roll up from a short side, using the paper to help. Trim the ends and cut the roulade into slices.

8. Serve garnished with salad leaves.

LEEK & PEPPER SLICE

SERVES 6

875 g (1¾ lb) small leeks, trimmed
400 g (14 oz) can pimientos, drained

VINAIGRETTE
2 tablespoons olive oil
1 tablespoon hazelnut oil
1 tablespoon white wine vinegar
salt and pepper to taste
1 tablespoon chopped mixed herbs, eg parsley, chives, tarragon

TO GARNISH
chopped parsley

1. Cook the leeks in boiling salted water until tender, about 10 minutes. Drain and immerse in cold water for 5 minutes; drain and dry thoroughly, squeezing to remove excess water. Dry the pimientos on kitchen paper and cut into thick strips.

2. Line a 1.2 litre (2 pint) terrine with foil, leaving an overlap at the edges.

3. Line the base of the terrine with a third of the leeks, packing them tightly. Cover with half of the pimiento strips. Continue these layers, finishing with leeks.

4. Fold the foil over the surface and weight down. (A small board with 2 or 3 food cans on top works well.) Chill overnight.

5. For the vinaigrette, whisk together the oils, vinegar, seasoning and herbs.

6. Carefully unmould the terrine and cut into slices. Serve drizzled with vinaigrette and sprinkled with chopped parsley.

ABOVE: CARROT ROULADE *BELOW*: LEEK & PEPPER SLICE

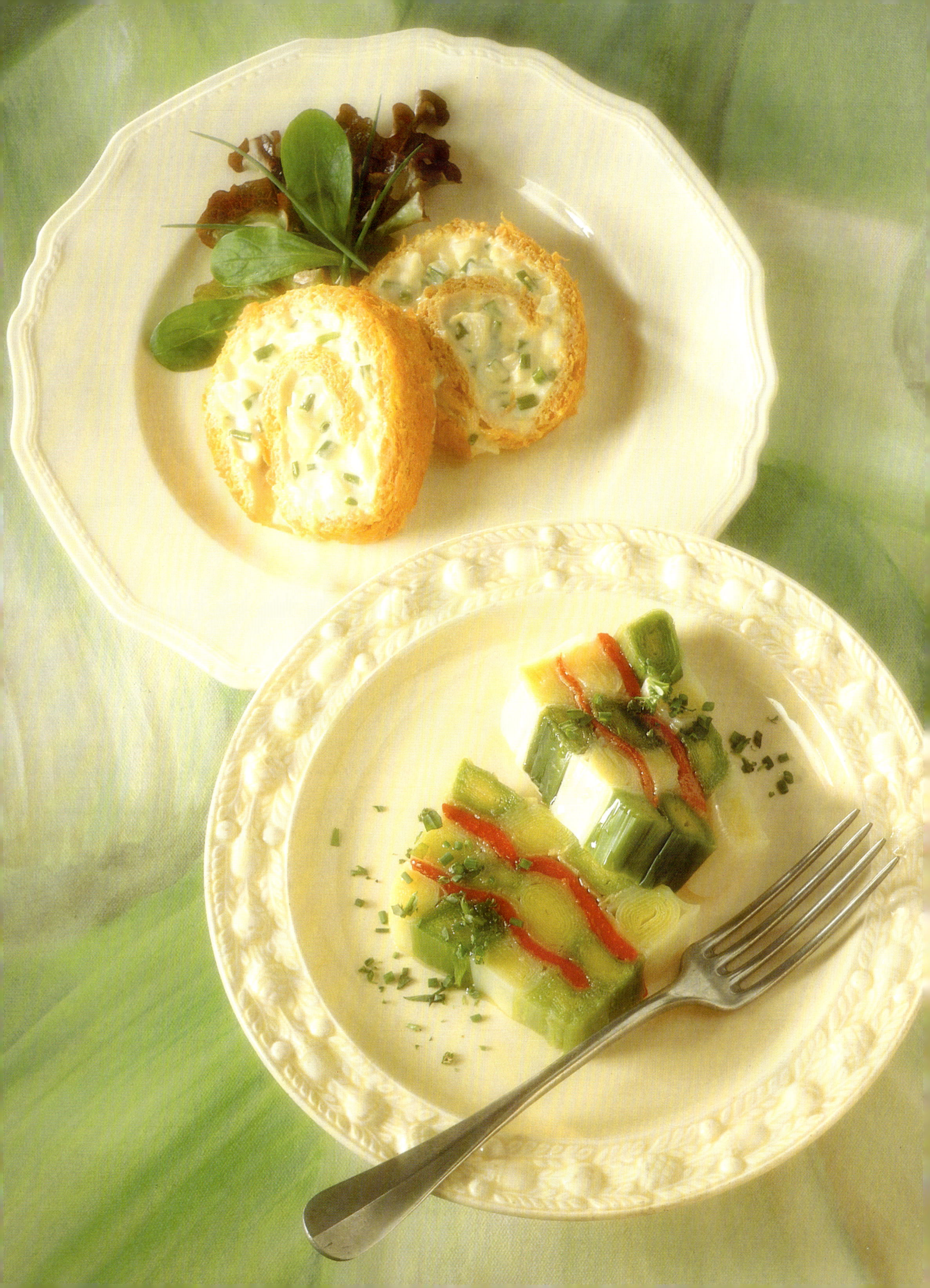

STARTERS

MUSHROOM RAGOÛT

SERVES 4

Find as many different types of mushrooms as you can to make this ragoût as flavoursome as possible.

50 g (2 oz) butter
2 shallots, finely chopped
500 g (1 lb) mixed mushrooms, eg shitake, oyster, chanterelles
4 tomatoes, peeled, seeded and diced
1 tablespoon chopped chives
salt and pepper to taste
2 tablespoons crème fraîche

TO SERVE
snipped chives
croûtes (fried bread) or toast

1. Melt the butter in a pan, add the shallots and cook until softened.

2. Add the mushrooms and cook, covered, for 5 minutes until softened and beginning to release liquid.

3. Stir in the tomatoes and chives. Simmer for a few seconds, until thickened. Season and stir in the crème fraîche.

4. Serve immediately, sprinkled with chives and accompanied by the croûtes or toast.

TOMATO SOUFFLÉS

SERVES 6

6 firm beef tomatoes
25 g (1 oz) butter
1 tablespoon tomato purée
1 teaspoon sugar
1 spring onion, finely chopped
salt and pepper to taste
15 g (½ oz) flour
125 ml (4 fl oz) hot milk
1 tablespoon freshly grated Parmesan cheese
2 eggs, separated
basil leaves to garnish

1. Preheat oven to 180°C (350°F/Gas 4).

2. Slice the top third off the tomatoes and discard. Using a teaspoon, scoop out the flesh, juice and seeds, reserving the flesh from 4 tomatoes. Leave tomatoes upside down on kitchen paper to drain.

3. Melt half the butter in a pan and add the reserved tomato flesh. Cook for 10-15 minutes until thickened. Add the tomato purée, sugar, spring onion and seasoning. Simmer for 2 minutes.

4. Melt remaining butter in another pan, stir in the flour and cook for 1 minute. Add the hot milk and cook, stirring, until very thick. Add to the tomato mixture with the Parmesan. Beat in the egg yolks.

5. Whisk the egg whites until soft peaks form and fold into the mixture.

6. Place the tomatoes on a baking sheet and fill with the soufflé mixture. Bake for 10-15 minutes until puffed and golden. Serve immediately, garnished with basil leaves.

ABOVE: MUSHROOM RAGOÛT *BELOW*: TOMATO SOUFFLÉS

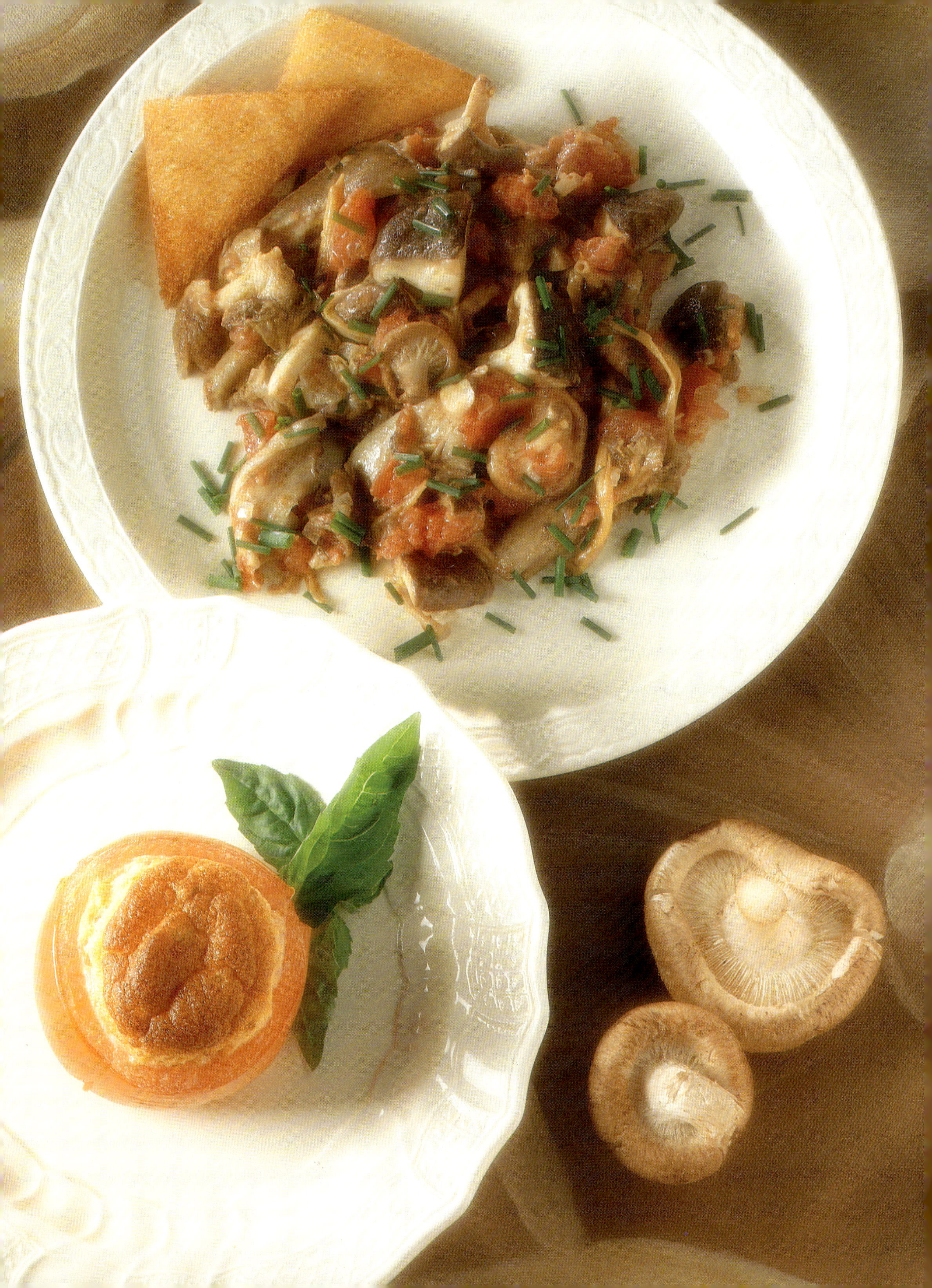

RATATOUILLE TARTLETS

SERVES 6

Ready-made filo pastry provides a quick way of making paper-light cases.

3 large sheets filo pastry, halved
2 tablespoons olive oil
2 cloves garlic, thinly sliced
2 courgettes, diced
1 small aubergine, diced
1 red pepper, cored, seeded and diced
2 spring onions, chopped
125 ml (4 fl oz) passata
1 teaspoon ground coriander
salt and pepper to taste
parsley sprigs to garnish

1 Preheat oven to 200°C (400°F/Gas 6). Pile the filo sheets on top of each other and cut into quarters.

2 Line 6 deep tartlet or muffin tins with the filo, using 4 squares for each, and arranging them at different angles to give a 'ragged' effect. Bake for 10 minutes, until golden.

3 Meanwhile, heat the oil in a sauté pan, add the garlic and fry until golden. Lift out with a slotted spoon and reserve.

4 Add the courgettes, aubergine and pepper to the pan and cook over a high heat until softened. Add the spring onions, passata, coriander and seasoning. Cook for a few seconds.

5 Fill the filo cases with the ratatouille and garnish with the sautéed garlic slivers and parsley to serve.

RED ONION & OLIVE TARTLETS

SERVES 6

250 g (8 oz) packet shortcrust pastry
350 g (12 oz) red onions, thinly sliced
1 tablespoon lemon juice
50 g (2 oz) butter
25 g (1 oz) raisins
1 tablespoon sugar
1 tablespoon balsamic or red wine vinegar
25 g (1 oz) black olives, quartered
salt and pepper to taste
salad leaves to garnish

1 Preheat oven to 200°C (400°F/Gas 6).

2 Roll out the pastry on a floured surface to a 3 mm (⅛ inch) thickness. Using a 9 cm (3½ inch) pastry cutter, stamp out six rounds and use to line 6 tartlet tins.

3 Prick the pastry bases, line with foil and fill with baking beans. Bake for 10 minutes, then remove foil and beans and bake for a further 10 minutes.

4 Meanwhile toss the sliced onions in the lemon juice. Melt the butter in a pan, add the onions and raisins, cover and cook gently until softened.

5 Add the sugar, vinegar and olives and cook for a further 5 minutes. Season with salt and pepper to taste.

6 Warm the pastry cases in the oven for a few minutes and fill with the onion mixture. Serve hot, garnished with salad leaves.

ABOVE: RATATOUILLE TARTLETS *BELOW:* RED ONION & OLIVE TARTLETS

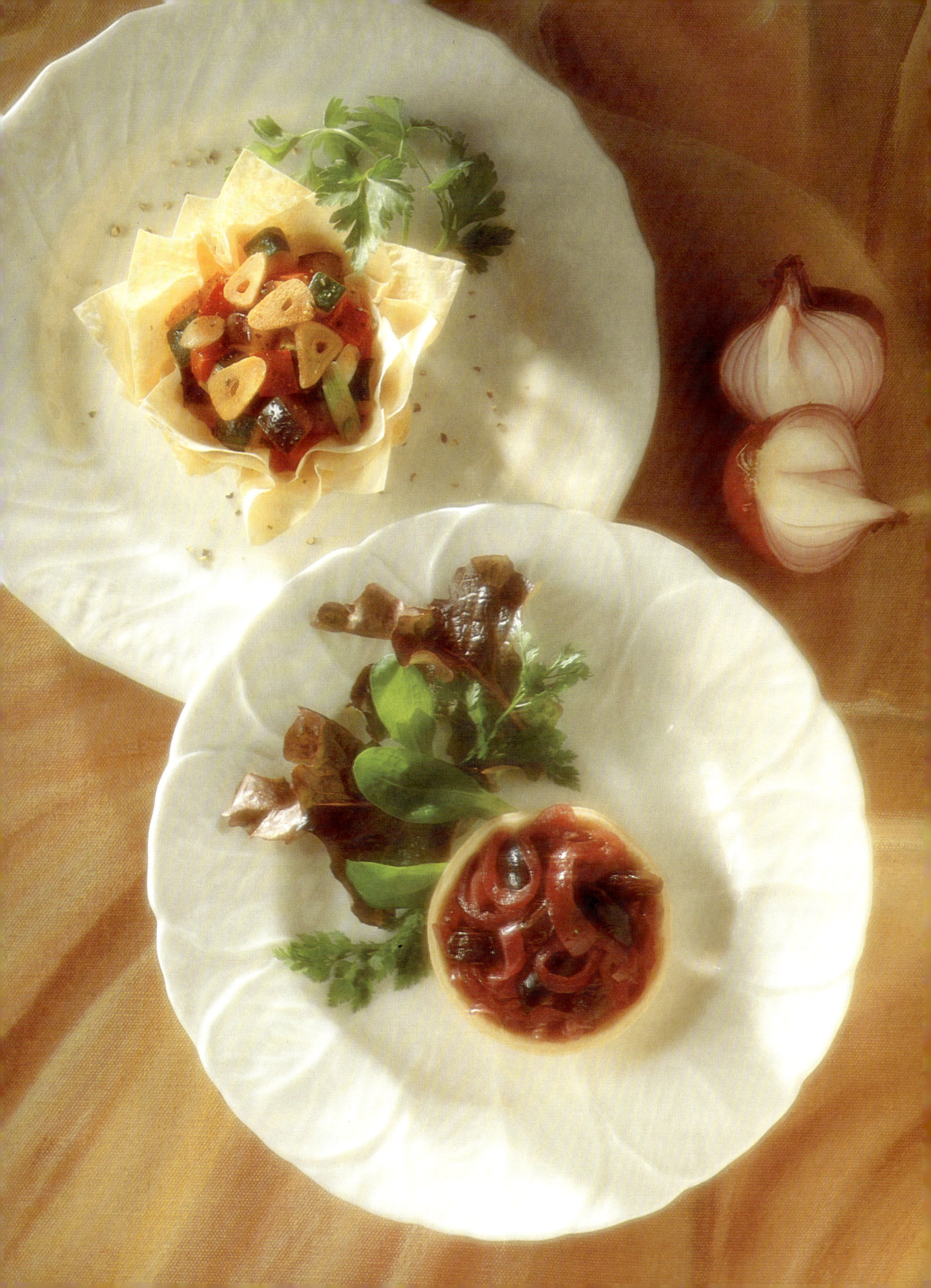

SPICED VEGETABLES IN POPPADUM CUPS

SERVES 4

150 ml (¼ pint) oil
1 aubergine, cubed
2 tablespoons chopped fresh root ginger
1 teaspoon dried crushed chillies
1 teaspoon cumin seeds
397 g (14 oz) can chopped tomatoes
1 tablespoon ground coriander
1 teaspoon turmeric
397 g (14 oz) can chick peas, drained
salt and pepper to taste
2 tablespoons chopped coriander
4 poppadums
1 teaspoon garam masala
coriander sprigs to garnish

1. Heat 6 tablespoons oil in a large frying pan. Add the aubergine and fry until soft and browned. Remove and set aside.

2. Heat remaining oil in the pan, add the ginger, chillies and cumin and fry for 1 minute. Add the tomatoes, ground coriander and turmeric. Cook for 10 minutes until thickened.

3. Add 300 ml (½ pint) water, bring to the boil, then add the aubergine, chick peas, seasoning and half the chopped coriander. Cover and simmer for 15 minutes.

4. Preheat grill to medium high and grill the poppadums until golden. Remove while still soft and gently mould each one over an upturned jar or tumbler. Leave to cool.

5. Add the remaining coriander and garam masala to the vegetable mixture. Spoon into the poppadum cups and serve garnished with coriander.

CRUDITÉS WITH PEPPER DIP

SERVES 4

Illustrated on back cover.

PEPPER DIP
2 red peppers, halved and seeded
1 clove garlic, crushed
½ red chilli, seeded
4 tablespoons olive oil
1 tablespoon chopped parsley
salt and pepper to taste

CRUDITÉS
8 asparagus spears, trimmed
1 large fennel bulb, trimmed
250 g (8 oz) cherry tomatoes
2 courgettes
1 head radicchio
50 g (2 oz) black olives

1. Preheat grill to high and grill the peppers, skin side up, until blackened and blistered. Remove and peel away the skins under running water; dry thoroughly.

2. Place the peppers in a food processor or blender with the garlic and chilli and work to a purée. With the motor running, slowly add the oil to yield a thick mixture. Add the parsley and seasoning. Transfer to a bowl.

3. Cook the asparagus in boiling salted water for 10-12 minutes, until tender. Drain and refresh in cold water.

4. Halve and slice the fennel. Slice the courgettes diagonally. Separate the radicchio leaves.

5. Arrange the vegetables and olives on a large serving platter with the dip.

RIGHT: SPICED VEGETABLES IN POPPADUM CUPS

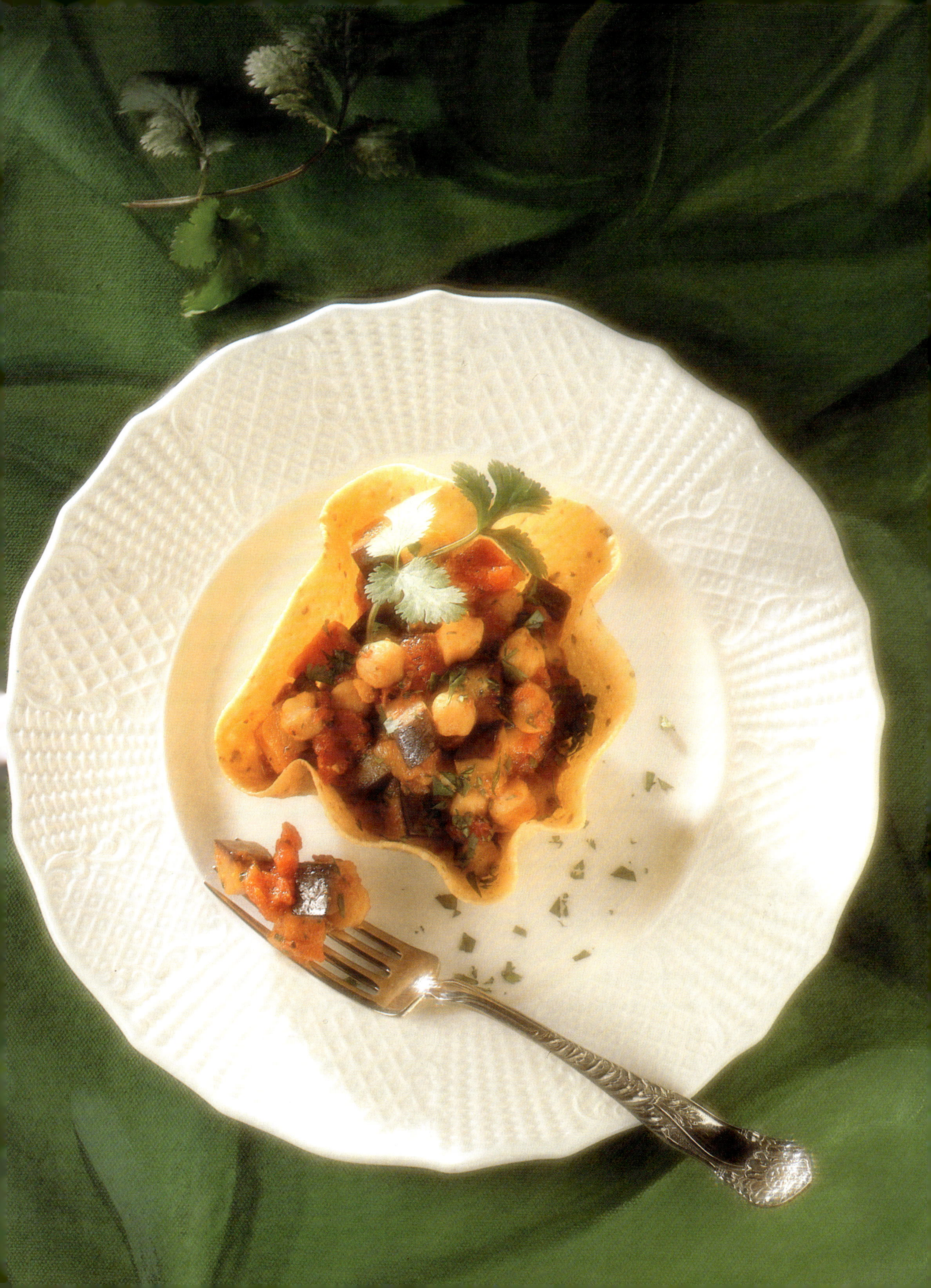

VEGETABLE TEMPURA

SERVES 4

The variety of vegetables you can use for this Japanese dish is endless.

1 red pepper, cored, seeded and cut into thick strips
1 courgette, in 1 cm (½ inch) slices
8 shitake or oyster mushrooms
50 g (2 oz) mangetout, trimmed
1 sweet potato, in 5 mm (¼ inch) slices
8 baby corn cobs
vegetable oil for deep-frying

BATTER
150 g (5 oz) plain flour
1 teaspoon baking powder
1 egg yolk
350 ml (12 fl oz) ice cold water

DIPPING SAUCE
3 tablespoons mirin (or medium sherry)
3 tablespoons light soy sauce
225 ml (8 fl oz) chicken stock
½ teaspoon chopped fresh root ginger

1. To make the batter, sift the flour and baking powder into a bowl. Mix the egg yolk with the water, then gradually add to the flour mixture, beating until smooth.

2. To make the sauce, gently heat the ingredients together in a pan; keep warm.

3. Half-fill a wok or deep pan with oil, and heat to 190°C (375°F). Dip the vegetables, a few at a time, into the batter and fry in the oil until lightly golden, about 1 minute. Drain on kitchen paper.

4. Serve the vegetable tempura immediately, with the dipping sauce.

SPICY GLASS NOODLE SALAD

SERVES 4

Cellophane noodles, also called glass noodles, are made from mung beans. Like dried cloud ear mushrooms, they are available from Oriental stores. You can use sliced button mushrooms instead of cloud ears if you prefer.

2 cloves garlic, crushed
1 tablespoon light soy sauce
4 tablespoons sugar
1 red chilli, seeded and finely sliced
1 tablespoon sesame oil
pepper to taste
150 g (5 oz) frozen prawns, defrosted
50 g (2 oz) cellophane noodles
1 carrot, cut into fine strips
1 courgette, cut into fine strips
5 dried cloud ear mushrooms, soaked in hot water until soft (optional)
1 tablespoon toasted sesame seeds

1. Mix together the garlic, soy sauce, sugar, chilli, sesame oil and pepper in a bowl. Add the prawns and toss well.

2. Cut the noodles into 10 cm (4 inch) lengths. Cook the noodles and carrot in boiling water for 1 minute. Add the courgette and cook for 1 minute. Drain and refresh in cold water. Drain thoroughly.

3. Place all the ingredients in a bowl and toss well to combine before serving.

ABOVE: VEGETABLE TEMPURA *BELOW:* SPICY GLASS NOODLE SALAD

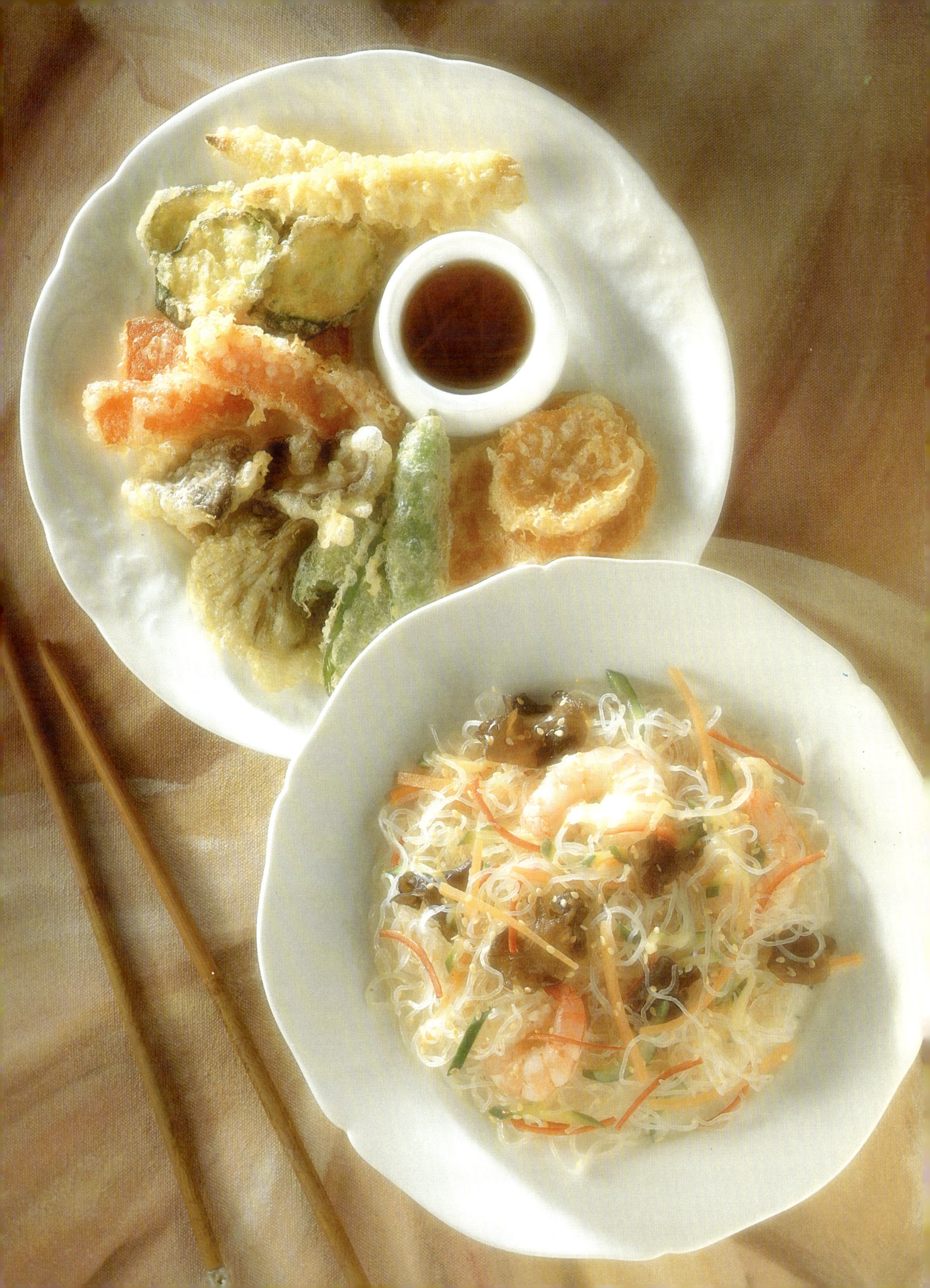

POTATO SKINS WITH HERB DIP

SERVES 4

Use a floury variety of potatoes, such as King Edwards. Cook the potatoes in the microwave for extra speed – allowing 10-12 minutes on high per 500 g (1 lb), turning occasionally.

4 medium baking potatoes
sunflower oil for brushing
salt and pepper to taste

DIP
125 ml (4 fl oz) low-fat fromage frais
2 tablespoons chopped chives
1 tablespoon chopped parsley

TO GARNISH
snipped chives

1. Preheat oven to 220°C (425°F/Gas 7).

2. Cook the potatoes in boiling salted water for 10-15 minutes until almost tender. Drain and cool.

3. Cut the potatoes into quarters and gently scrape out most of the flesh, leaving a 1 cm (½ inch) layer. Cut in half again.

4. Place the potato 'skins' on a baking tray, brush with a little oil and sprinkle with salt and pepper. Bake for 15-20 minutes until golden.

5. For the dip, mix together the fromage frais, chives and parsley in a small bowl. Season with salt and pepper. Sprinkle with chives.

6. Serve the hot potato skins with the herb dip.

GUACAMOLE

SERVES 4-6

Fresh coriander makes this Mexican avocado dip truly authentic. Served with corn chips or crudités, it makes a good party dish. Use tabasco if fresh chillies are unavailable.

2 large ripe avocados, peeled and chopped
1 small onion, chopped
3 ripe tomatoes, chopped
juice of 1 lime
1 green chilli, seeded and chopped
1 tablespoon chopped coriander leaves
salt and pepper to taste

TO SERVE
coriander sprigs
chilli slices
corn chips

1. Place the avocados, onion, tomatoes, lime juice, chilli and coriander in a food processor or blender and work to a rough purée.

2. Season with salt and pepper.

3. Transfer to a serving bowl and garnish with coriander and chilli. Serve the guacamole with corn chips.

ABOVE: POTATO SKINS WITH HERB DIP BELOW: GUACAMOLE

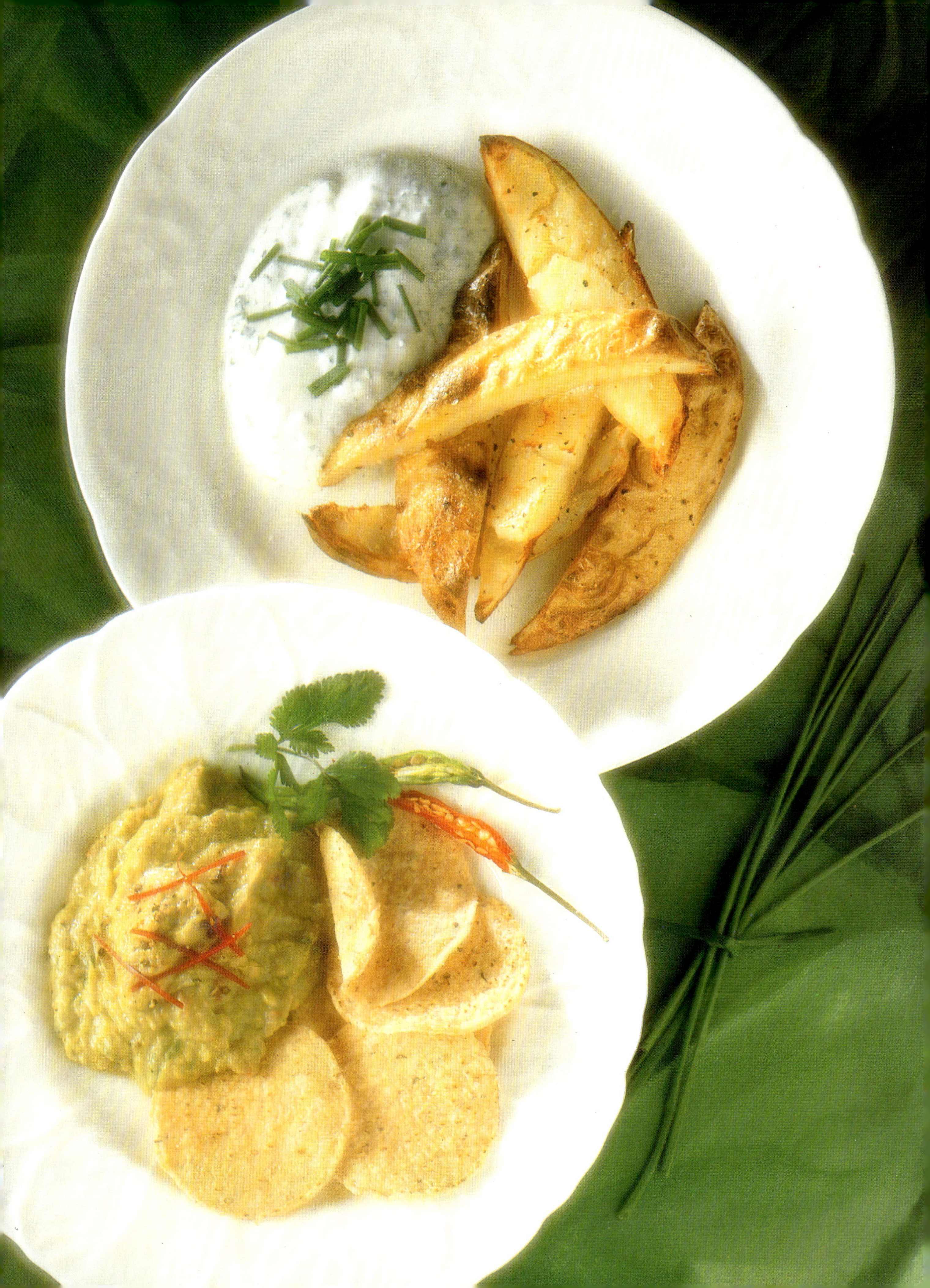

SOUPS

Vegetables lend themselves perfectly to soups – whether you use one variety or a combination with complementary flavours. Vary the textures by using chunky pieces of vegetables, small pasta and pulses. For cream soups, purée in a blender or food processor then pass through a sieve for a velvety smooth result. Home-made soups freeze successfully – simply package in empty waxed milk cartons, allowing a little space at the top for expansion. Defrost quickly by microwave.

To serve, garnish your soup with a swirl of cream, yogurt or fromage frais and finish with a sprinkling of chopped fresh herbs, croûtons or toasted nuts.

CONTENTS

WATERCRESS & LIME SOUP	28
THAI-STYLE HOT & SOUR SOUP	28
TOMATO & PIMIENTO SOUP	30
ROCKET SOUP WITH PARMESAN	30
PEA & MINT SOUP	32
CURRIED PUMPKIN SOUP	32
TUSCAN BEAN SOUP	34
PISTOU VEGETABLE SOUP	34
WHITE GAZPACHO	36
BEETROOT & FENNEL SOUP	36

WATERCRESS & LIME SOUP

SERVES 6

This soup is equally delicious served hot or cold. Don't overcook the watercress, or it will lose its colour.

50 g (2 oz) butter
250 g (8 oz) potato, diced
250 g (8 oz) leek, chopped
3 bunches watercress, stalks removed
1 litre (1¾ pints) chicken stock
salt and pepper to taste
grated rind and juice of 1 lime
4 tablespoons cream
watercress sprigs to garnish

1. Melt the butter in a large pan. Add the potato and leek, and cook gently for about 10 minutes until soft.

2. Meanwhile finely chop the watercress. Add the chicken stock to the pan, bring to the boil and add a pinch of salt. Add the watercress and simmer for 8 minutes.

3. Transfer to a food processor or blender and purée until smooth.

4. Return the soup to the pan. Add the lime rind and juice, check the seasoning and heat through.

5. Transfer to individual soup plates, swirl in the cream and serve garnished with watercress.

THAI-STYLE HOT & SOUR SOUP

SERVES 6

This soup uses typical Thai ingredients – dried lemon grass and straw mushrooms – available from larger supermarkets. Use button mushrooms, if you prefer.

1.5 litres (2½ pints) chicken stock
2 tablespoons dried lemon grass
1 tablespoon grated lime rind
salt to taste
3 tablespoons lime juice
¼ teaspoon chilli paste
¼ teaspoon sugar
½ ×425 g (15 oz) can straw mushrooms, drained
125 g (4 oz) beansprouts
1 bunch spring onions, thinly sliced
250 g (8 oz) frozen prawns, defrosted
2 small red chillies, seeded and thinly sliced
3 tablespoons coriander leaves

1. Put the stock, lemon grass and lime rind in a large pan. Bring to the boil, lower the heat and simmer gently for 15 minutes.

2. Strain the stock and return to the pan. Season with salt, then add the lime juice, chilli paste and sugar. Stir well.

3. Add the mushrooms, beansprouts and spring onions. Simmer for 1 minute.

4. Add the prawns and simmer for a few seconds to heat through.

5. Serve in individual bowls, sprinkled with chilli slices and coriander leaves.

ABOVE: WATERCRESS & LIME SOUP BELOW: THAI-STYLE HOT & SOUR SOUP

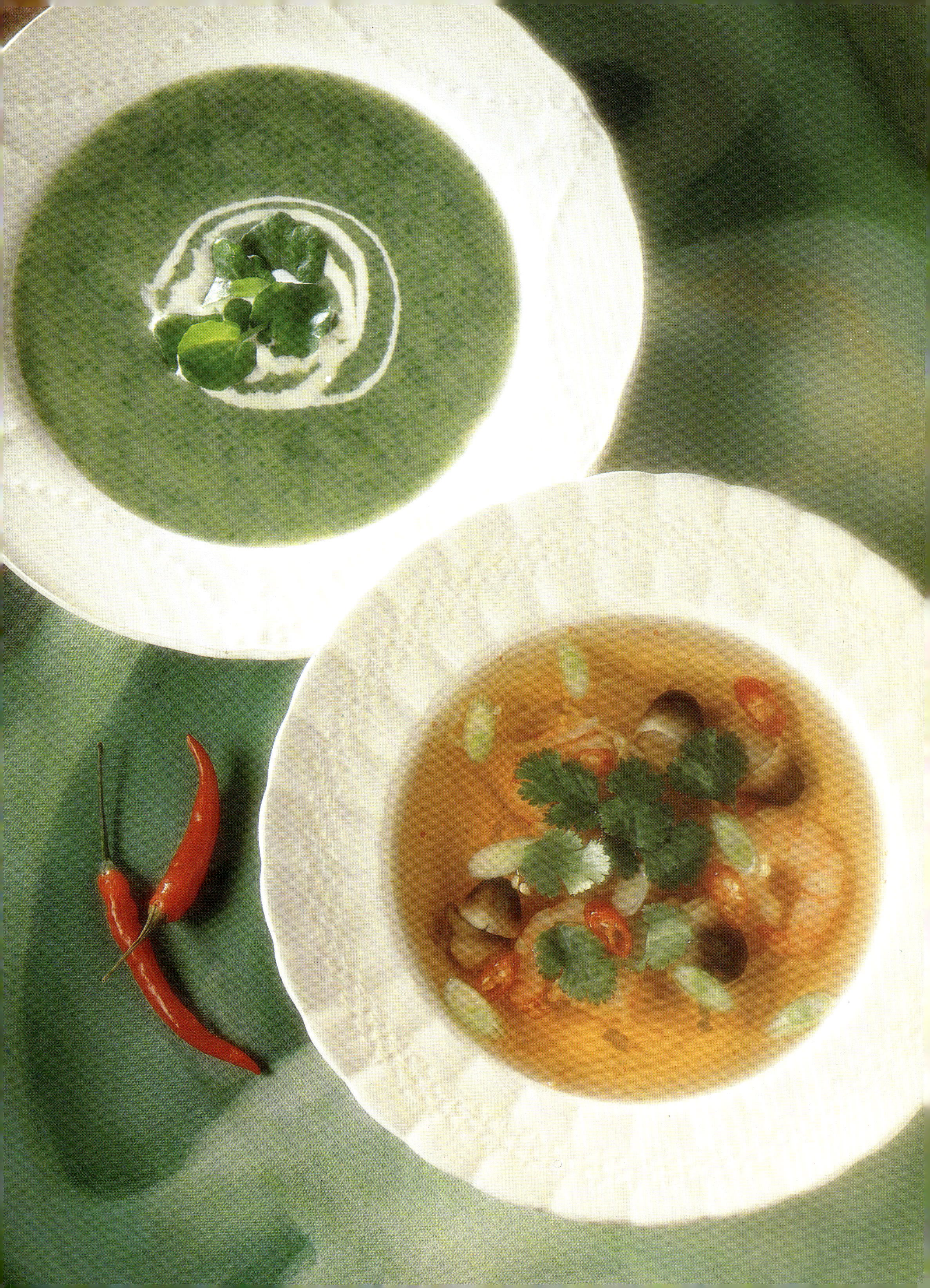

TOMATO & PIMIENTO SOUP

SERVES 4

A very quick 'storecupboard' recipe – perfect for an impromptu dinner party.

50 g (2 oz) butter
1 onion, finely chopped
2 cloves garlic, crushed
400 g (14 oz) can pimientos, drained, rinsed and chopped
230 g (8 oz) can chopped tomatoes
150 ml (¼ pint) red wine
600 ml (1 pint) chicken stock
salt and pepper to taste
2 tablespoons snipped chives

CROÛTONS
2 slices white bread, crusts removed
2 tablespoons oil

1. Melt half the butter in a pan. Add the onion and garlic and cook until soft.

2. Add the pimientos and tomatoes, cover and cook gently for 10 minutes.

3. Add the wine, cook for 5 minutes, then add the stock and cook for 5 minutes.

4. Transfer to a food processor or blender and purée until smooth. Return the soup to the pan, season and heat through.

5. To make the croûtons, cut the bread into small cubes. Heat the remaining butter and the oil in a frying pan, then fry the bread cubes until golden. Drain on kitchen paper.

6. Transfer the soup to individual bowls and garnish with the chives and croûtons to serve.

ROCKET SOUP WITH PARMESAN

SERVES 4-6

Rocket is a salad leaf with a superb pungent, peppery taste. Substitute watercress, if you can't obtain it.

2 tablespoons quality olive oil
2 cloves garlic, crushed
250 g (8 oz) potato, diced
175 g (6 oz) rocket, chopped
1.2 litres (2 pints) vegetable stock
salt and pepper to taste
4 tablespoons freshly grated Parmesan cheese
¼ teaspoon dried crushed chillies (optional)

1. Heat the olive oil in a large pan. Add the garlic and cook for 1 minute.

2. Add the potato and stir until coated in oil. Add the rocket, reserving a few leaves for garnish. Stir and cook for 2-3 minutes.

3. Heat the stock and add to the rocket mixture. Season with salt and pepper, cover and simmer for 20 minutes.

4. Ladle into soup bowls and sprinkle with Parmesan, and dried chilli if desired. Garnish with rocket leaves to serve.

ABOVE: TOMATO & PIMIENTO SOUP   *BELOW*: ROCKET SOUP WITH PARMESAN

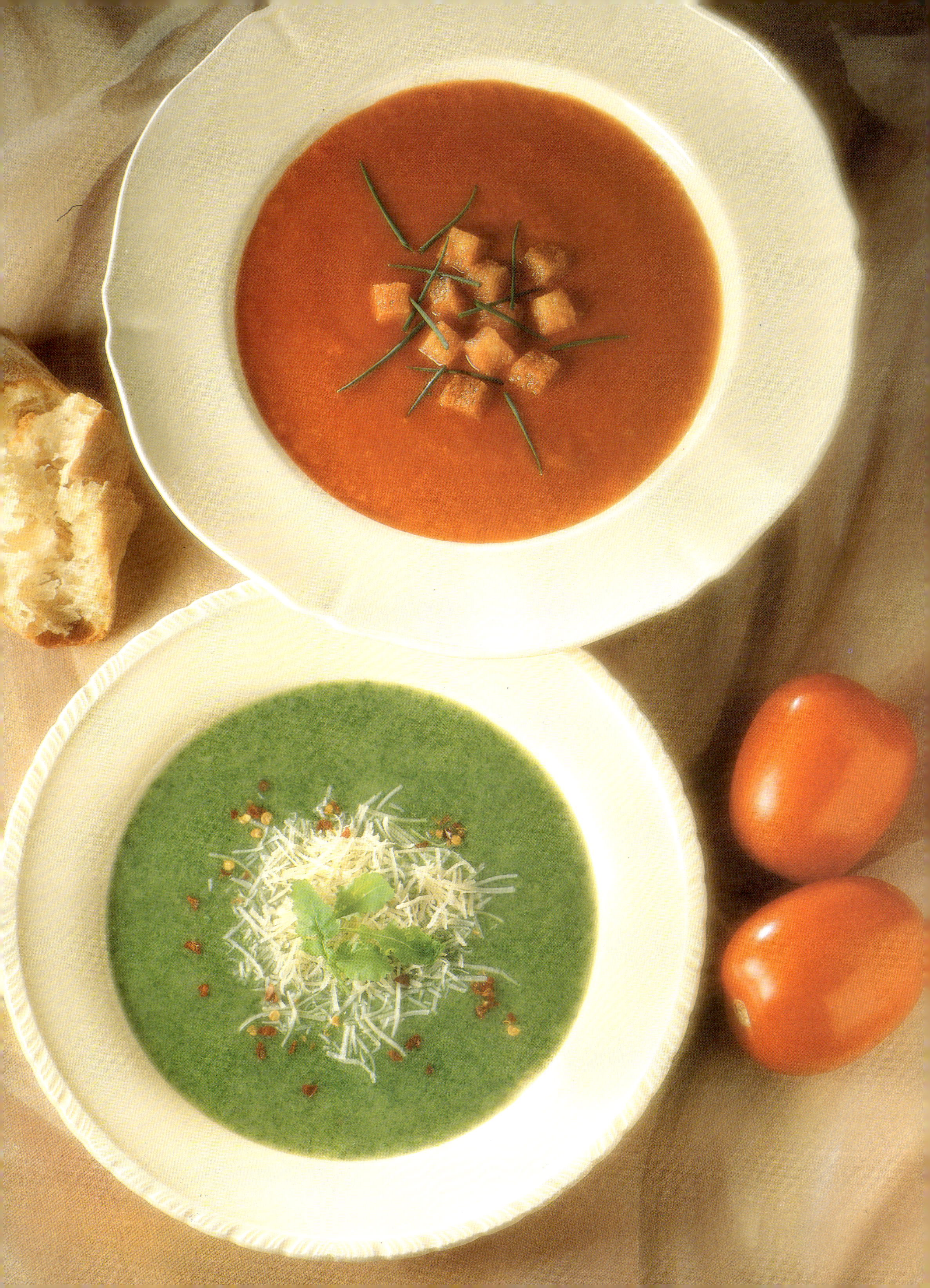

PEA & MINT SOUP

SERVES 6

50 g (2 oz) butter
1 bunch spring onions, chopped
3 tablespoons flour
900 ml (1½ pints) chicken stock
1 teaspoon salt
300 g (10 oz) frozen peas
500 g (1 lb) sugar snap peas, trimmed
600 ml (1 pint) water
8 lettuce leaves
25 g (1 oz) mint leaves
salt and white pepper to taste
125 ml (4 fl oz) cream

TO GARNISH
few lettuce leaves, shredded
mint sprigs

1. Melt the butter in a large pan. Add the spring onions and cook for 3-4 minutes until tender. Stir in the flour and cook, stirring, for 1 minute. Stir in the chicken stock, salt and frozen peas. Cover and cook for 10 minutes.

2. Transfer to a food processor or blender and purée until smooth. Return to the pan.

3. Put the sugar snaps, water, lettuce and mint leaves in a pan. Bring to the boil, cover and simmer for 15 minutes. Purée in the food processor or blender, then sieve to remove any strings.

4. Add to the spring onion and pea mixture, stir in the cream, season and reheat.

5. Serve garnished with lettuce and mint.

CURRIED PUMPKIN SOUP

SERVES 4

To cook this soup ultra quickly in the microwave, cook the onion, garlic and oil on high for 1 minute. Add the remaining ingredients, except yogurt, and cook for a further 5 minutes.

2 tablespoons oil
1 onion, chopped
1 clove garlic, crushed
1 tablespoon mild curry paste
425 g (15 oz) can pumpkin, drained
600 ml (1 pint) chicken stock
salt and pepper to taste
4 tablespoons natural yogurt
coriander sprigs to garnish

1. Heat the oil in a large pan. Add the onion and garlic, and cook until soft. Add the curry paste and cook for a few seconds, stirring.

2. Add the pumpkin and chicken stock. Stir well, season and simmer for 15-20 minutes.

3. Transfer the soup to a food processor or blender and purée until smooth. Return to the pan, check the seasoning and reheat.

4. Transfer to individual soup plates, swirl in the yogurt and garnish with coriander.

ABOVE: PEA & MINT SOUP *BELOW:* CURRIED PUMPKIN SOUP

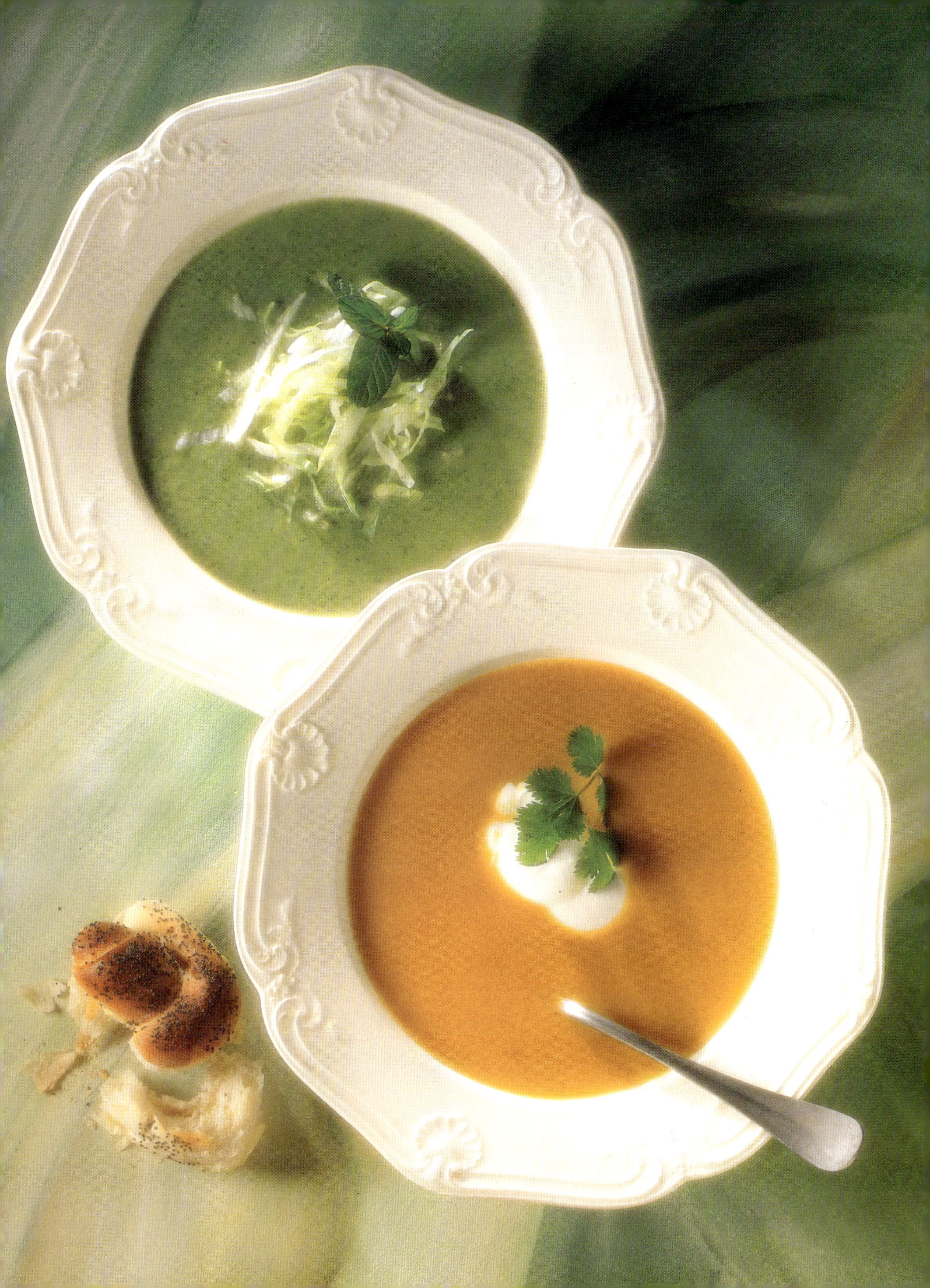

TUSCAN BEAN SOUP

SERVES 4

A soup for garlic lovers! If haricot beans are unavailable, you can use canned cannellini or flageolet beans instead.

2 × 435 g (15 oz) cans haricot beans
1 litre (1¾ pints) vegetable stock
salt and pepper to taste
150 ml (¼ pint) quality olive oil
4 cloves garlic, thinly sliced
25 g (1 oz) chopped parsley
parsley sprigs to garnish

1. Drain the haricot beans, rinse well and drain. Put half of them in a large pan with the vegetable stock. Bring to the boil, cover and simmer for 10-15 minutes.

2. Transfer to a food processor or blender and purée until smooth, adding a little water if the soup is too thick. Return to the pan, season and add the remaining whole beans. Reheat.

3. Heat 4 tablespoons of the olive oil in a separate pan and fry the garlic slices until golden. Add to the soup with the remaining oil and chopped parsley.

4. Serve garnished with parsley sprigs.

PISTOU VEGETABLE SOUP

SERVES 4-6

Use small pasta stars or shells and cut the vegetables into small chunks to allow them to cook quickly. Red pesto contains sun-dried tomatoes – adding a delicious flavour to this hearty soup.

1 courgette, diced
50 g (2 oz) potato, diced
50 g (2 oz) onion, chopped
1 carrot, diced
230 g (8 oz) can chopped tomatoes
salt and pepper to taste
1.2 litres (2 pints) boiling water (approximately)
50 g (2 oz) French beans, cut into 1 cm (½ inch) lengths
50 g (2 oz) frozen petit pois
50 g (2 oz) small pasta shapes
4-6 tablespoons red pesto
freshly grated Parmesan cheese to serve

1. Place the courgette, potato, onion, carrot and tomatoes in a large pan. Add seasoning and enough boiling water to cover generously. Simmer for 20 minutes.

2. Add the French beans, petit pois and pasta. Cook for 10 minutes until the pasta is tender. Check the seasoning.

3. Transfer the soup to individual soup plates, adding a tablespoon of pesto to each. Serve with grated Parmesan cheese.

ABOVE: TUSCAN BEAN SOUP   *BELOW*: PISTOU VEGETABLE SOUP

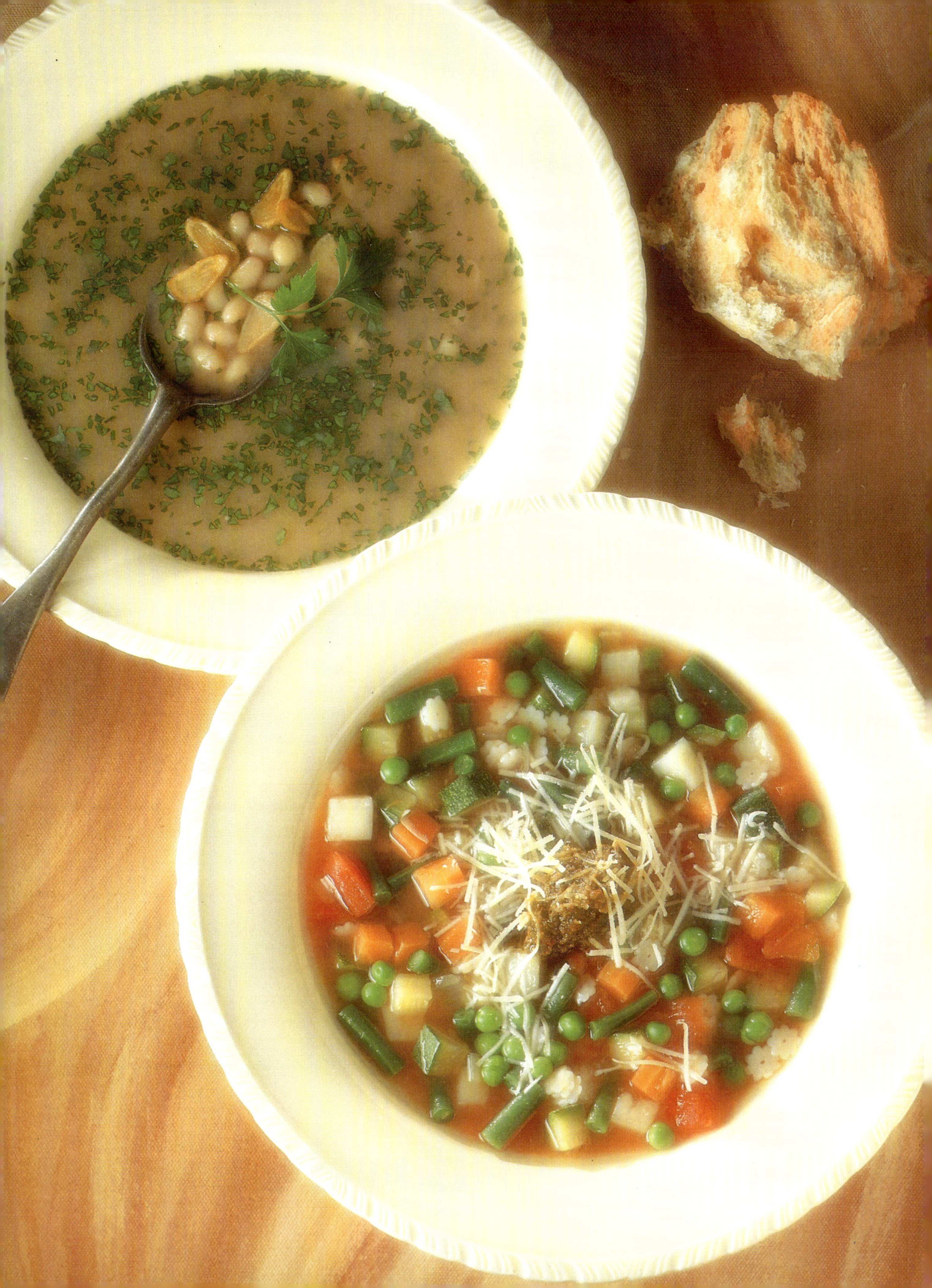

WHITE GAZPACHO
SERVES 6

A pretty summer soup. Either make it well in advance to give adequate time to chill, or add a few ice cubes when serving.

2 cucumbers, peeled and diced
1 clove garlic
1 green pepper, diced
750 ml (1¼ pints) chicken stock
425 ml (15 fl oz) thick sour cream
225 ml (8 fl oz) natural yogurt
3 tablespoons white wine vinegar
2 teaspoons salt
pepper to taste

TO GARNISH
parsley sprigs
diced cucumber and green pepper
toasted flaked almonds

1. Place the cucumbers, garlic and green pepper in a food processor or blender with a little of the chicken stock. Purée until smooth, then add the remaining stock.

2. Put the sour cream and yogurt into a bowl and stir in a little of the puréed mixture to thin.

3. Stir in the remaining mixture, and add the vinegar, salt and pepper. Chill.

4. Serve garnished with parsley and accompanied by bowls of diced cucumber, green pepper and flaked almonds.

BEETROOT & FENNEL SOUP
SERVES 4

Chicken consommé gives this soup a good rich flavour, but you can use stock instead. Serve hot or chilled.

50 g (2 oz) butter
250 g (8 oz) fennel, thinly sliced
425 g (15 oz) can chicken consommé
125 ml (4 fl oz) red wine
350 g (12 oz) cooked beetroot, chopped
salt and pepper to taste
2 tablespoons chopped dill
4 tablespoons thick sour cream

TO GARNISH
dill sprigs
shredded cooked beetroot

1. Melt the butter in a pan. Add the fennel and cook gently until softened.

2. Add the chicken consommé and red wine. Bring to the boil, cover and simmer for 5 minutes. Add the beetroot and cook for 10 minutes.

3. Transfer to a food processor or blender and purée until smooth. Season and stir in the dill.

4. If serving chilled, allow the soup to cool, then chill for several hours. If serving hot, reheat gently.

5. Add a spoonful of sour cream to each serving and garnish with dill and beetroot.

ABOVE: WHITE GAZPACHO *BELOW:* BEETROOT & FENNEL SOUP

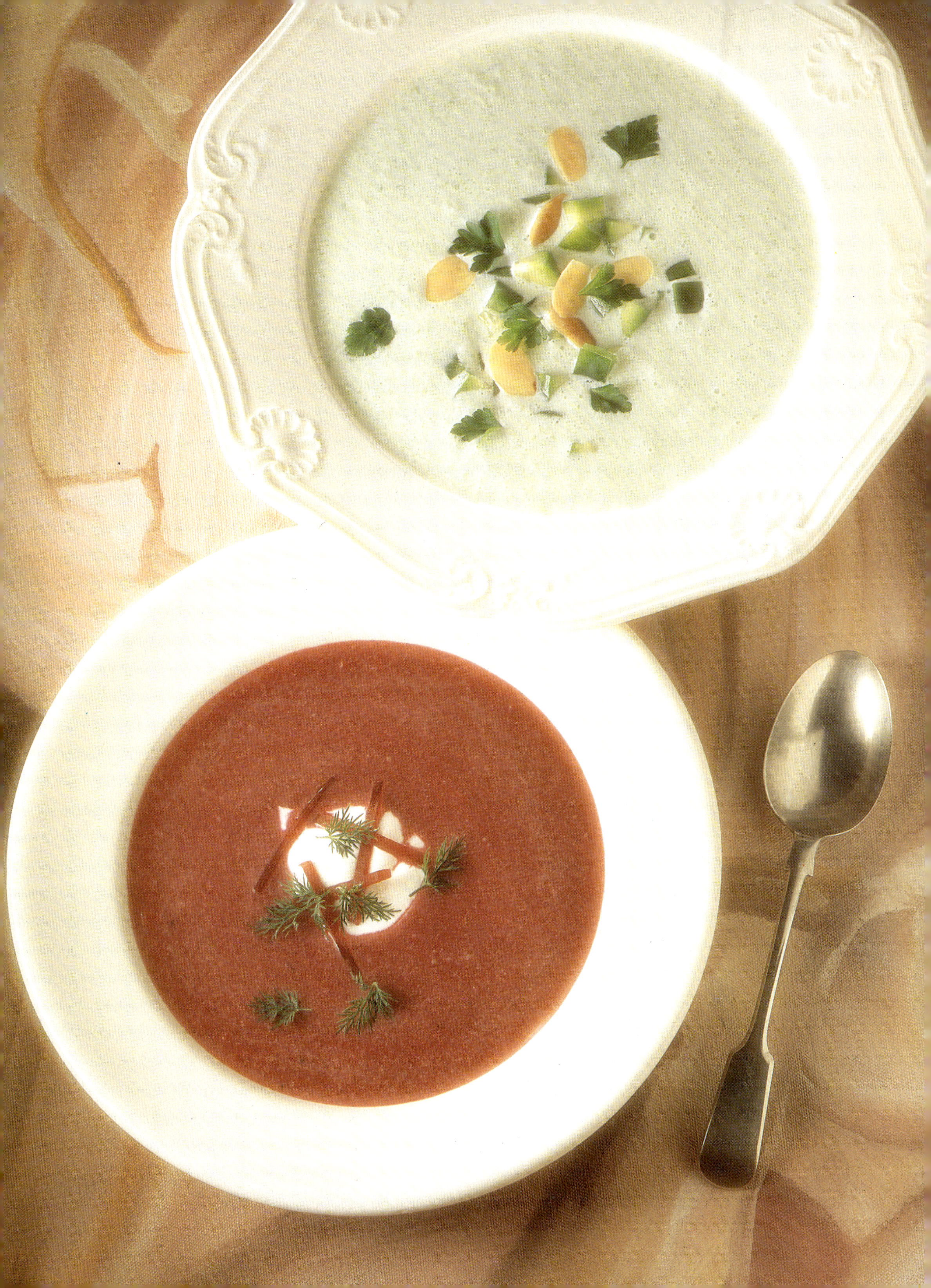

MAIN COURSES

With the trends towards healthier eating and vegetarianism, main courses based on vegetables are becoming increasingly popular. Vegetables are, of course, full of vitamins and fibre. Combine them with pulses or grains, and you have a nutritious, satisfying meal.

These recipes include Italian, French and African influences - offering a varied collection to choose from. Many can be served in smaller portions as starters or tasty snacks, especially the gnocchi, pizza, and leek tart. Served with rice, potatoes, pasta or salad, however, every recipe provides a substantial main course.

CONTENTS

SPINACH & HAM CRÊPES	40
SPINACH & HERB EGGAH	42
FRITTATA	42
STUFFED SQUASH	44
GNOCCHI WITH ROCKET SAUCE	44
ONION & GRUYÈRE JALOUSIE	46
PEPPER & AUBERGINE PIZZA	48
LEEK & GOAT'S CHEESE TART	48
VEGETABLE COUSCOUS	50
PASTA WITH BROCCOLI & ANCHOVIES	52
PASTA WITH RICOTTA, MUSHROOMS & BACON	52
PRAWN GUMBO	54
ARTICHOKE RISOTTO	56
PRAWN & MANGETOUT STIR-FRY	56
CHICKEN & MUSHROOM GOUGÈRE	58
CHILLI BEAN & SAUSAGE STEW	60
VEGETABLE POT-AU-FEU	60

SPINACH & HAM CRÊPES

SERVES 4

Cooked pancakes freeze very successfully, and can be filled with a variety of savoury mixtures. Try adding chopped fresh herbs to the batter, before cooking.

130 g (4½ oz) packet batter mix
2 eggs
125 g (4 oz) butter
250 g (8 oz) ricotta cheese
salt and pepper to taste
grated nutmeg to taste
500 g (1 lb) frozen chopped spinach, defrosted
4 tablespoons freshly grated Parmesan cheese
8 large thin slices ham

TO SERVE
225 ml (8 fl oz) passata
parsley sprigs to garnish

1. Preheat oven to 230°C (450°F/Gas 8).

2. Make up the batter according to the packet instructions (see note). Beat in the eggs to yield a smooth batter.

3. Melt a knob of butter in a small frying pan. When sizzling, pour in enough batter to thinly coat the base of the pan, tilting the pan to spread the batter evenly. Cook for 1 minute, then using a palette knife, turn the crêpe over. Cook the underside until lightly browned. Repeat this process until you have 8 crêpes, layering them between pieces of greaseproof paper as they are cooked, to prevent them sticking.

4. In a bowl, mix together 25 g (1 oz) of the butter, the ricotta cheese, salt, pepper, and nutmeg. Squeeze the spinach to remove as much moisture as possible, then add to the mixture. Stir in half of the Parmesan cheese.

5. Lay a slice of ham on each crêpe, then spread with the spinach mixture to within 1 cm (½ inch) of the edges. Roll up the crêpes and cut each one in half.

6. Layer the crêpes in a buttered ovenproof dish, and sprinkle with the remaining Parmesan. Dot with the remaining butter.

7. Bake for 20 minutes until golden brown. Meanwhile, season the passata with salt and pepper and heat through in a small pan.

8. Serve the spinach and ham crêpes garnished with sprigs of parsley and accompanied by the seasoned passata.

NOTE:
If you prefer, make up your own quick crêpe batter in a blender or food processor. Simply process 150 g (5 oz) plain flour, a pinch of salt, 225 ml (8 fl oz) milk and 150 ml (¼ pint) water with the 2 eggs from the recipe, until smooth.

RIGHT: SPINACH & HAM CRÊPES

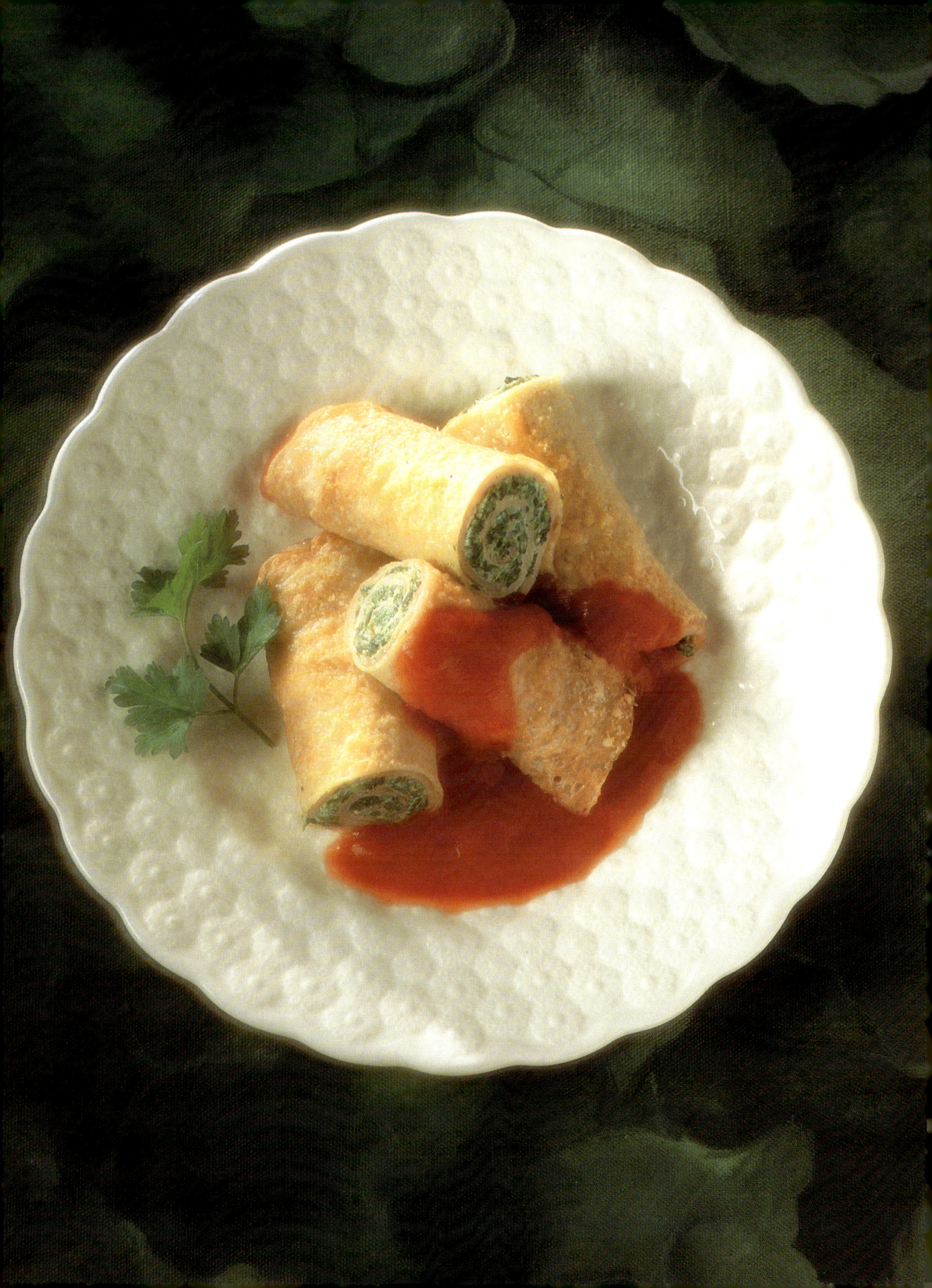

SPINACH & HERB EGGAH

SERVES 4

This is a Middle Eastern omelette. As a variation, try a filling of diced cooked chicken flavoured with spices and pine nuts.

6 eggs
2 leeks, finely chopped
125 g (4 oz) frozen chopped spinach, defrosted and squeezed dry
5 spring onions, chopped
3 tablespoons chopped parsley
3 tablespoons chopped dill or coriander
75 g (3 oz) chopped walnuts
salt and pepper to taste
15 g (½ oz) butter

TO SERVE
coriander sprigs
cherry tomatoes
Greek-style yogurt

1. Preheat oven to 180°C (350°F/Gas 4).

2. Beat the eggs in a large bowl. Stir in the leeks, spinach, spring onions, herbs, walnuts and seasoning.

3. Grease a 25 cm (10 inch) round ovenproof dish with the butter and pour in the mixture. Bake for 30 minutes, covering with foil if the top browns too quickly.

4. Serve warm or cold, cut into wedges. Garnish with coriander and tomatoes, and serve with yogurt.

FRITTATA

SERVES 4

This Italian baked omelette is good served hot or cold. Cut into fingers, it makes perfect party food.

4 tablespoons olive oil
1 large onion, sliced
1 red pepper, cored, seeded and sliced
1 green pepper, cored, seeded and sliced
2 courgettes, sliced
3 cloves garlic, thinly sliced
4 eggs, beaten
salt and pepper to taste
90 ml (3 fl oz) milk
basil leaves to garnish

1. Preheat oven to 200°C (400°F/Gas 6).

2. Heat the olive oil in a frying pan. Add the onion and peppers and cook until soft. Transfer to an oiled 20-23cm (8-9 inch) ovenproof dish, using a slotted spoon.

3. Add the courgettes to the frying pan and sauté until tender and golden. Add to the onion and peppers.

4. Sauté the garlic slices in the frying pan until softened. Add to the vegetables.

5. Season the eggs with salt and pepper and stir in the milk. Pour over the vegetables and mix lightly to distribute evenly.

6. Dot the top with a few basil leaves, reserving some for garnish. Bake for 25-30 minutes, until set and golden brown.

7. Garnish with the remaining basil and serve hot or cold, cut into squares.

ABOVE: SPINACH & HERB EGGAH   BELOW: FRITTATA

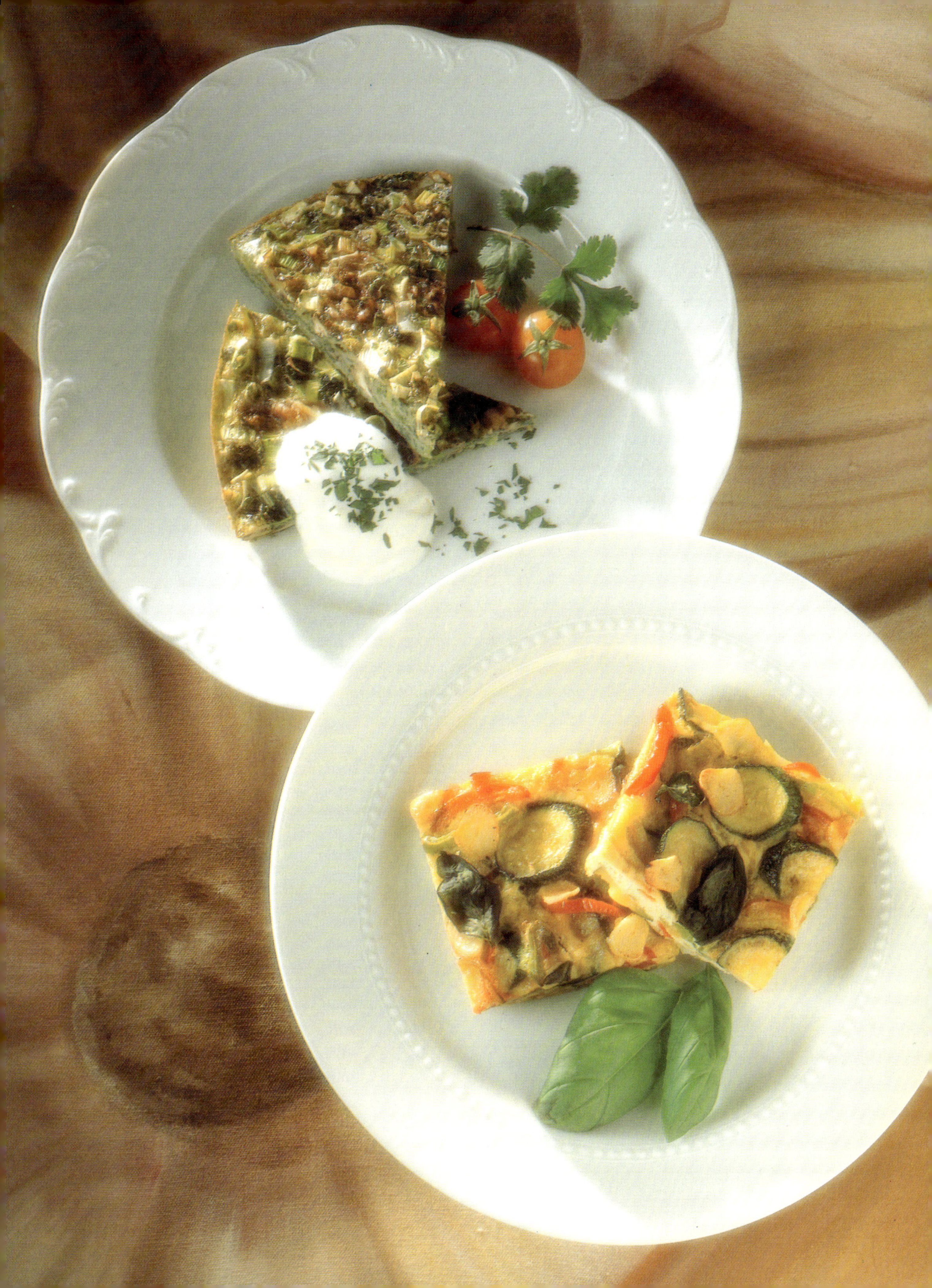

MAIN COURSES

STUFFED SQUASH

SERVES 4

Choose small even-sized summer squashes, such as round courgettes or patty pans.

8 squashes, each about 175 g (6 oz)
salt and pepper to taste
50 g (2 oz) butter
1 small onion, finely chopped
1 clove garlic, crushed
250 g (8 oz) lean beef, minced
230 g (8 oz) can chopped tomatoes
1 tablespoon chopped fresh root ginger
½ teaspoon ground cinnamon
1 tablespoon raisins
1 tablespoon pine nuts

1. Cook the squashes in boiling salted water until tender; 15-20 minutes, depending on size. Alternatively, cook in the microwave for 6-8 minutes. Drain.

2. Slice off the tops of the squash for lids. Scoop out the flesh, leaving 5 mm (¼ inch) thick shells. Chop the flesh.

3. Preheat oven to 200°C (400°F/Gas 6).

4. Melt the butter in a pan, add the onion and garlic and cook until softened.

5. Add the meat and fry, stirring, until browned. Add the tomatoes, ginger, seasoning, cinnamon, raisins and nuts; simmer for 10-15 minutes. Stir in the chopped squash.

6. Fill the squashes with stuffing, replace the lids and place in a roasting tin, containing 2.5 cm (1 inch) water. Bake for 10 minutes, until hot. Serve with Greek yogurt and a side salad.

GNOCCHI WITH ROCKET SAUCE

SERVES 4

Try this Italian favourite, made simpler by using instant mashed potato.

125 g (4 oz) instant mashed potato
salt and pepper to taste
grated nutmeg to taste
125 g (4 oz) plain flour, sifted
60 ml (2 fl oz) white wine
20 g (¾ oz) rocket, finely chopped
150 ml (5 fl oz) double cream
25 g (1 oz) butter
2 tablespoons freshly grated Parmesan cheese
rocket leaves to garnish

1. Cook potato according to the quick method packet instructions. Add seasoning and nutmeg. Let cool for a few minutes. Add the flour and mix until smooth.

2. With floured hands, shape the potato mixture into 2 cm (¾ inch) thick rolls. Cut into 2.5 cm (1 inch) lengths. Mark with the back of a fork.

3. Bring a large pan of salted water to the boil and cook the gnocchi, in batches of 10, for about 10 seconds. Lift out with a slotted spoon and place in a warm dish.

4. Simmer the wine until reduced by half. Add the rocket and cream and boil for 3 minutes, until slightly thickened. Off the heat, whisk in the butter and seasoning.

5. Pour the sauce over the gnocchi and sprinkle with Parmesan. Garnish with rocket leaves and serve immediately.

ABOVE: STUFFED SQUASH *BELOW*: GNOCCHI WITH ROCKET SAUCE

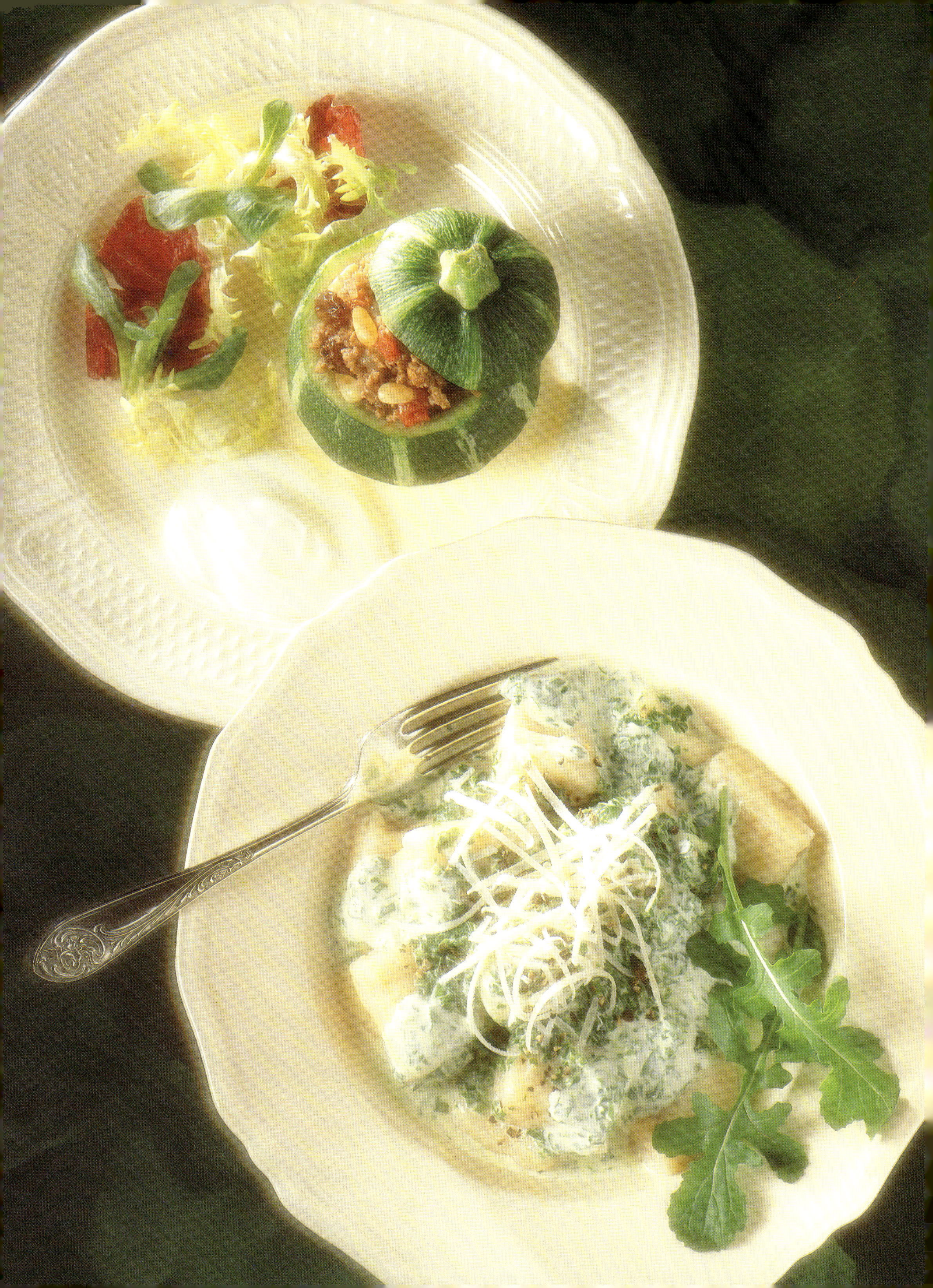

MAIN COURSES

ONION & GRUYÈRE JALOUSIE

SERVES 4-6

The top of this attractive pie is slashed to represent a venetian blind – the literal translation of the French word 'jalousie'. Ready-made puff pastry is available fresh or frozen.

50 g (2 oz) butter
3 large onions, thinly sliced
1 tablespoon wholegrain mustard
salt and pepper to taste
350 g (12 oz) packet puff pastry
25 g (1 oz) gruyère cheese, grated
beaten egg to glaze
2 teaspoons sesame seeds
salad leaves to garnish

1. Preheat oven to 230°C (450°F/Gas 8).

2. Melt the butter in a large pan, add the onions and cook gently until softened. Stir in the mustard and seasoning.

3. Divide the pastry into 2 pieces, one slightly larger than the other. Roll out the pastry on a floured surface to 2 rectangles, the smaller measuring about 20×13 cm (8×5 inches); the larger one measuring 25×18 cm (10×7 inches).

4. Place the smaller rectangle on a dampened baking sheet and top with the onion mixture. Spread evenly, leaving a 1 cm (½ inch) border all the way round. Sprinkle the cheese over the onion filling.

5. Dust the other pastry rectangle with flour and gently fold it in half. Using a sharp knife, cut through the folded side, at 5 mm (¼ inch) intervals, leaving a 2.5 cm (1 inch) border at the sides and top. Open out the rectangle.

6. Brush the pastry border around the onion with water, then carefully lay the cut pastry rectangle on top. Press the edges together to seal and crimp with your fingers.

7. Brush the jalousie with beaten egg and sprinkle with sesame seeds. Bake for 20 minutes, until well risen and golden brown.

8. Cut into thick slices and serve warm, garnished with salad leaves.

RIGHT: ONION & GRUYÈRE JALOUSIE

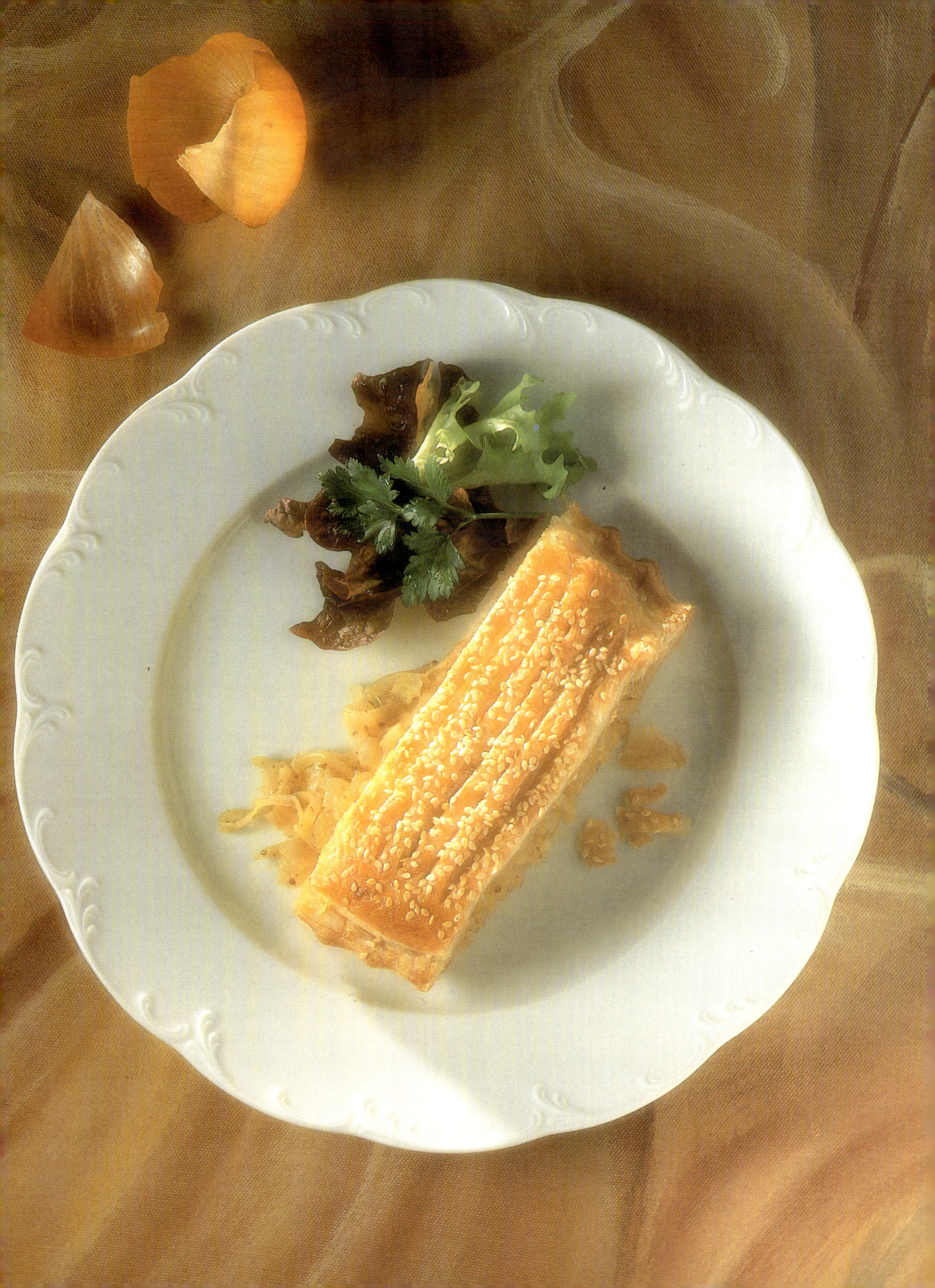

PEPPER & AUBERGINE PIZZA

SERVES 4

290 g (10.2 oz) packet pizza base mix
125 ml (4 fl oz) passata
1 aubergine, thinly sliced
2 tomatoes, thinly sliced
1 red pepper, cored, seeded and thinly sliced
1 yellow pepper, cored, seeded and thinly sliced
1 onion, thinly sliced
2 tablespoons capers
12 black olives
50 g (1.76 oz) can anchovies, drained
2 × 150 g (5 oz) mozzarella cheeses
pepper to taste
olive oil for drizzling
oregano sprigs to garnish

1. Preheat oven to 220°C (425°F/Gas 7).

2. Make up the pizza base mix according to packet instructions. (For speed, use a food processor.)

3. Divide the dough into 4 equal pieces. On a floured surface, roll out each piece to a thin circle, 18 cm (7 inches) in diameter.

4. Place on lightly greased baking sheets and turn up the edges slightly.

5. Spread each one with passata, leaving a 5 mm (¼ inch) border. Top with the aubergine, tomatoes, peppers, onion, capers, olives and anchovies. Slice or chop the mozzarella and dot over the pizzas. Season with pepper and drizzle with olive oil.

6. Bake for 20 minutes until golden brown. Garnish with oregano to serve.

LEEK & GOAT'S CHEESE TART

SERVES 4-6

For a quicker method, cook the filling in the flan case without pre-baking. The pastry won't be as crisp, but is satisfactory if eaten immediately.

350 g (12 oz) packet shortcrust pastry
50 g (2 oz) butter
500 g (1 lb) leeks, thinly sliced
salt and pepper to taste
1 egg
1 egg yolk
150 ml (¼ pint) single cream
1 teaspoon dried oregano
100 g (3½ oz) mild goat's cheese
50 g (2 oz) walnut pieces

1. Preheat oven to 190°C (375°F/Gas 5).

2. Roll out the pastry on a floured surface and use it to line a 20-23 cm (8-9 inch) tart tin. Prick the base with a fork. Line with foil, fill with baking beans and bake for 10-15 minutes. Remove foil and beans.

3. Melt the butter in a large pan, add the leeks and cook until softened. Season and allow to cool for a few minutes.

4. Beat together the egg, yolk and cream. Add to the leeks with the oregano. Crumble in the goat's cheese.

5. Fill the pastry case with the leek mixture. Top with the walnuts. Bake for 20 minutes until golden.

6. Serve warm, cut into wedges, with a mixed leaf salad.

ABOVE: PEPPER & AUBERGINE PIZZA *BELOW:* LEEK & GOAT'S CHEESE TART

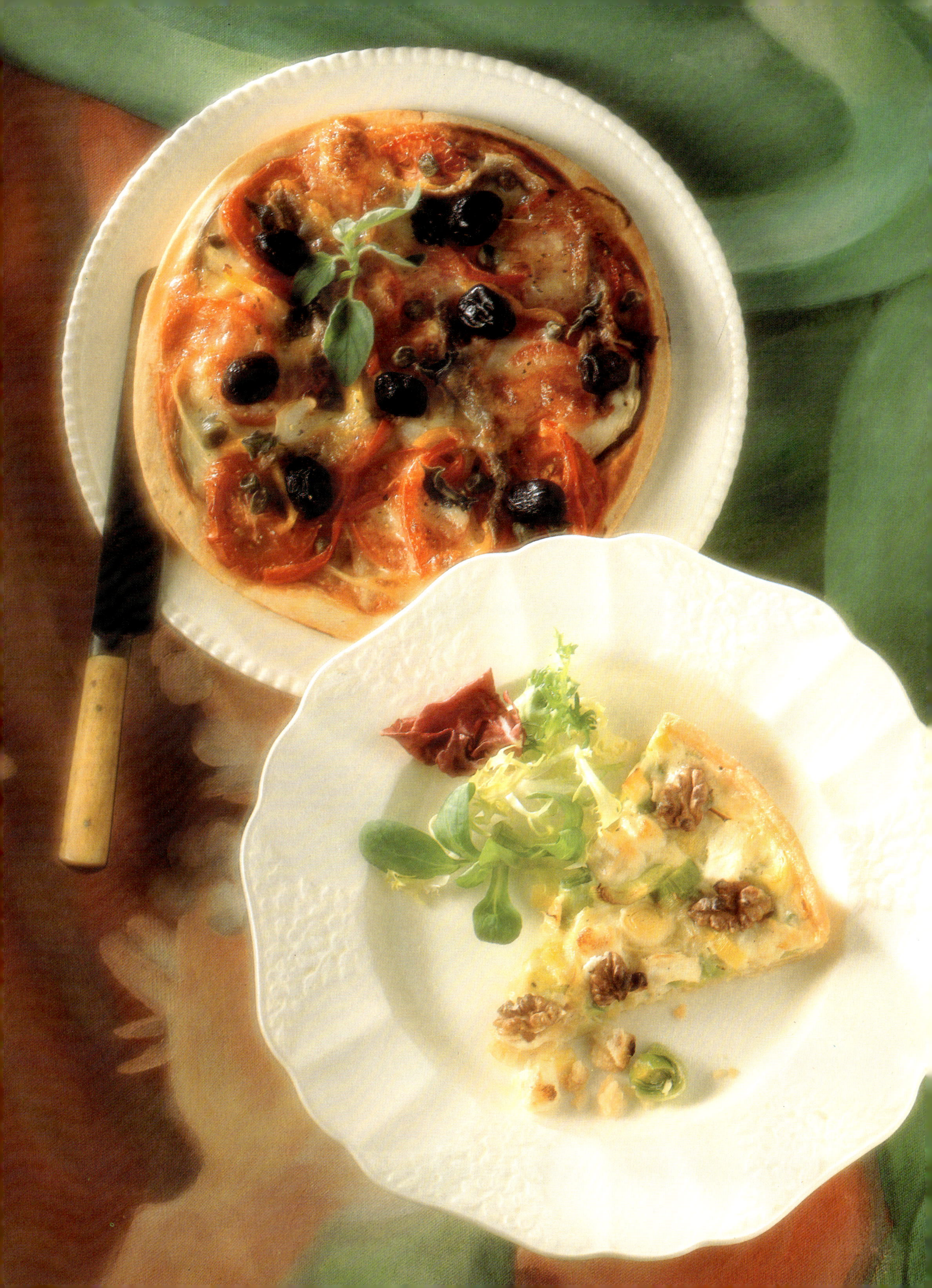

VEGETABLE COUSCOUS

SERVES 6

Couscous is a cereal processed from semolina and used in North Africa as an alternative to rice. It makes a delicious base for this sustaining spiced vegetable mixture.

3 tablespoons oil
1 teaspoon salt
500 g (1 lb) couscous
50 g (2 oz) butter
1 large onion, finely chopped
2 cloves garlic, crushed
1 tablespoon tomato purée
½ teaspoon turmeric
½ teaspoon cayenne pepper
1 teaspoon ground coriander
1 teaspoon ground cumin
250 g (8 oz) cauliflower florets
250 g (8 oz) baby carrots, trimmed
1 red pepper, cored, seeded and diced
250 g (8 oz) courgettes, thickly sliced
250 g (8 oz) baby corn
250 g (8 oz) button mushrooms, halved
3 tablespoons chopped coriander
salt and pepper to taste
coriander leaves to garnish

1 Bring 500 ml (18 fl oz) water to the boil in a large pan. Add 1 tablespoon oil and the salt. Remove from the heat, then add the couscous, stirring. Allow to swell for 2 minutes, then add the butter and heat gently, stirring to separate the grains; keep hot.

2 Heat the remaining 2 tablespoons oil in a large pan, add the onion and garlic, and fry until softened. Stir in the tomato purée, turmeric, cayenne, ground coriander and cumin. Cook, stirring, for 2 minutes.

3 Add the cauliflower, carrots and pepper and enough water to come halfway up the vegetables. Bring to the boil and simmer, covered, for 10 minutes.

4 Add the courgettes and baby corn and cook for a further 10 minutes. Add the mushrooms, chopped coriander and seasoning. Cook for 2-3 minutes.

5 Turn the couscous out on to a serving dish and spoon the vegetables on top, pouring over any extra liquid. Garnish with coriander leaves.

RIGHT: VEGETABLE COUSCOUS

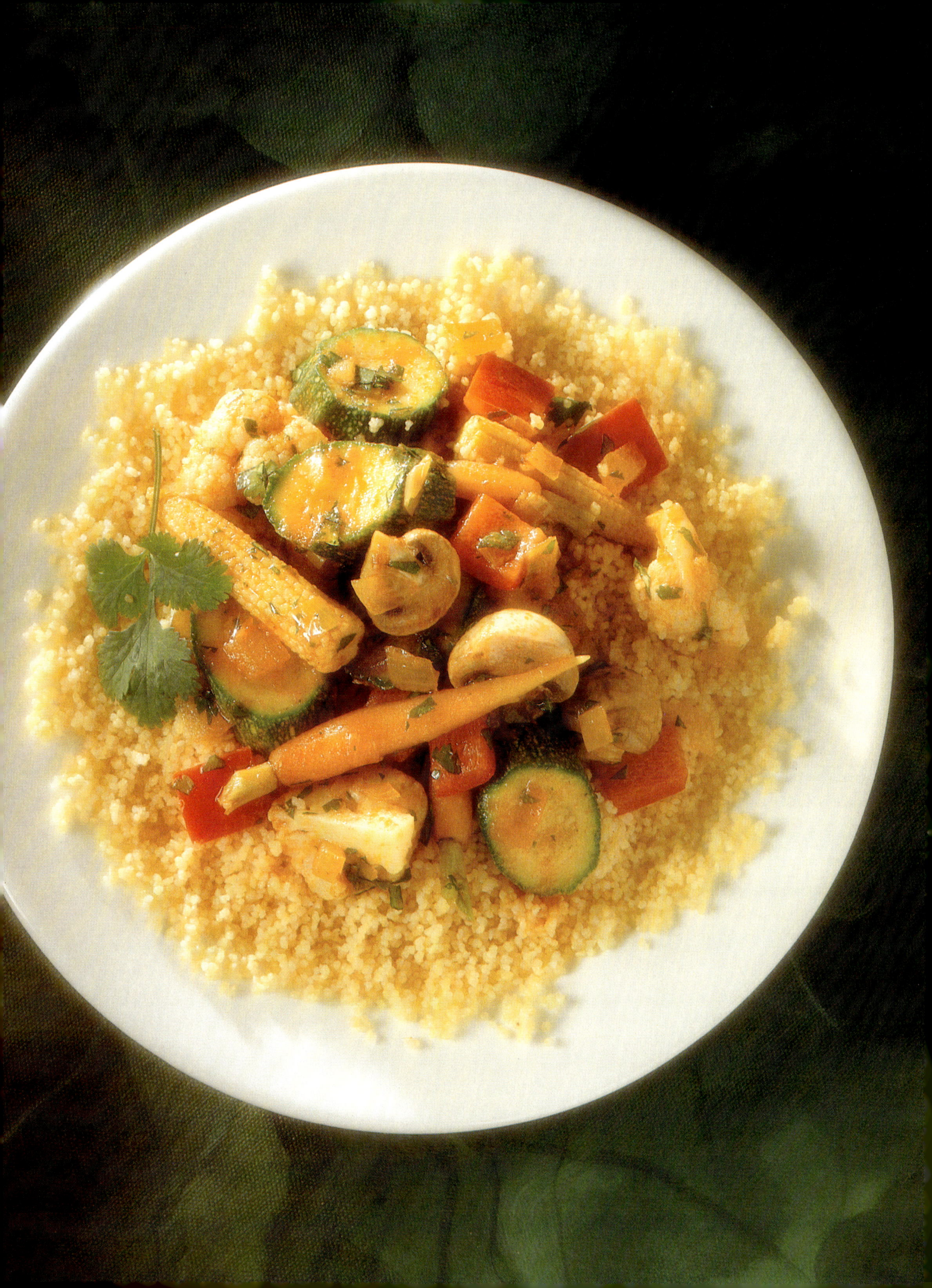

PASTA WITH BROCCOLI & ANCHOVIES

SERVES 4

You can use other pasta shapes for this dish, but the sauce adheres particularly well to pasta spirals.

500 g (1 lb) pasta spirals
salt and pepper to taste
350 g (12 oz) broccoli florets
4 tablespoons olive oil
1 red pepper, cut into strips
50 g (1.76 oz) can anchovies, drained and chopped
25 g (1 oz) butter
125 g (4 oz) freshly grated Parmesan cheese

1. Cook the pasta in plenty of boiling salted water for 10-12 minutes, until *al dente*, tender but firm to the bite.

2. Meanwhile, cook the broccoli florets in boiling salted water for about 6 minutes. Drain.

3. Heat the olive oil in a frying pan, add the pepper and cook until slightly softened. Add the anchovies and continue cooking until they break up and dissolve. Add the broccoli and half of the butter. Season with pepper and cook for a further few minutes.

4. Drain the pasta, return to the pan and add the broccoli mixture, together with the remaining butter and Parmesan cheese. Toss well and serve immediately.

PASTA WITH RICOTTA, MUSHROOMS & BACON

SERVES 4

If ricotta is unavailable, use cottage cheese as a substitute. Flat mushrooms have the most pronounced flavour of the cultivated varieties.

500 g (1 lb) pasta shells
25 g (1 oz) butter
12 rashers smoked streaky bacon, derinded and chopped
350 g (12 oz) flat mushrooms, finely chopped
350 g (12 oz) ricotta cheese
salt and pepper to taste
2 tablespoons chopped parsley
parsley sprigs to garnish

1. Cook the pasta in plenty of boiling salted water for 10-12 minutes, until tender but firm to the bite.

2. Melt the butter in a pan, add the bacon and fry gently until golden brown and slightly crisp. Add the mushrooms and cook, stirring, until all the liquid has evaporated.

3. Stir in the ricotta cheese, seasoning and chopped parsley.

4. Drain the pasta, return to the pan and stir in the mushroom mixture.

5. Serve immediately, garnished with parsley.

ABOVE: PASTA WITH BROCCOLI & ANCHOVIES *BELOW*: PASTA WITH RICOTTA, MUSHROOMS & BACON

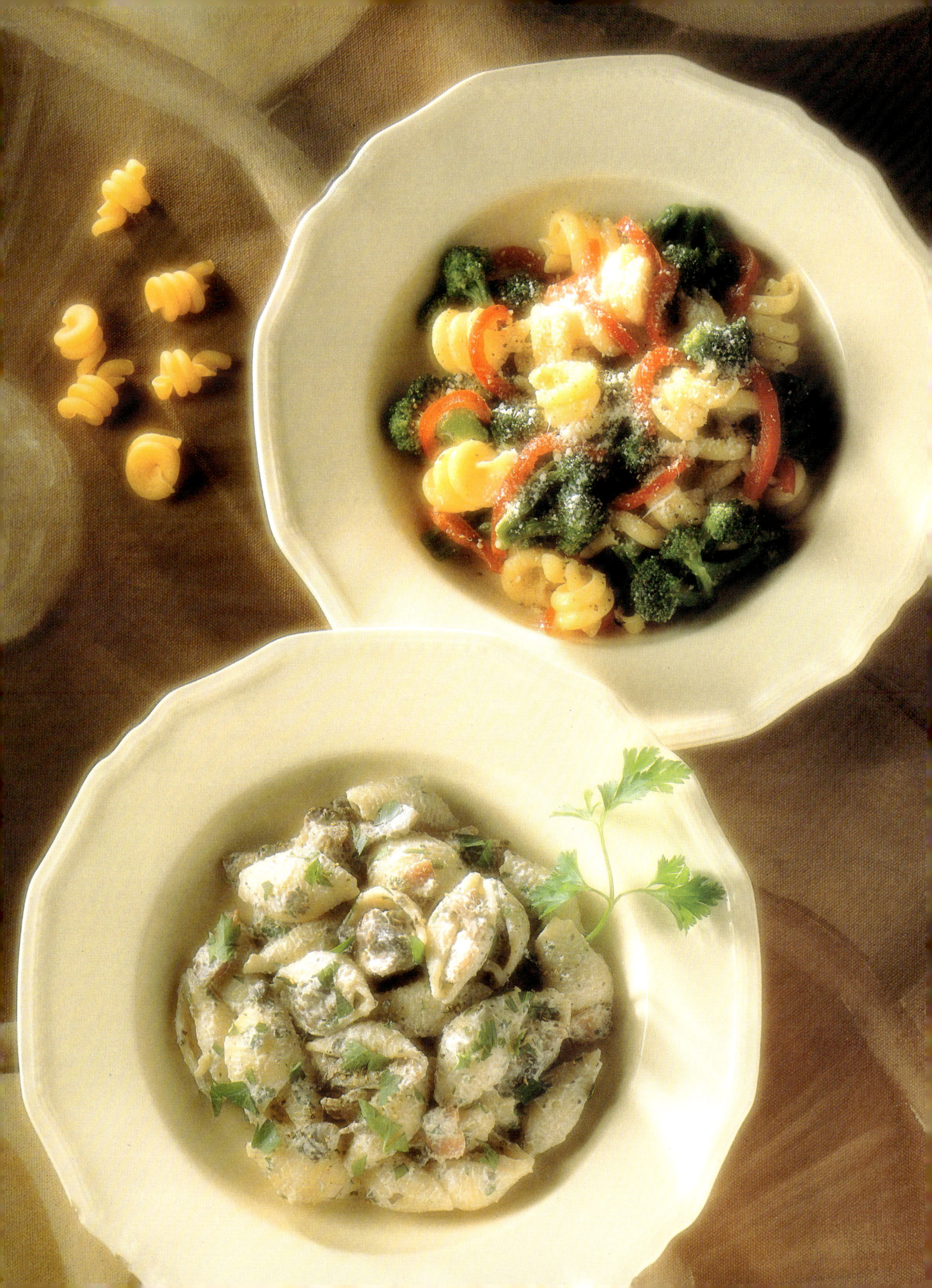

CREOLE PRAWN GUMBO

SERVES 6

This tasty Creole dish is a cross between a stew and a soup. It is traditionally served with rice. The most important ingredient is okra, a bright green seed pod, which gives the dish its characteristic silky texture. Use fresh or defrosted frozen prawns.

125 g (4 oz) butter
60 g (2½ oz) plain flour
1 onion, chopped
1 green pepper, cored, seeded and chopped
2 spring onions, chopped
1 tablespoon chopped parsley
1 clove garlic, crushed
1 beef tomato, chopped
100 g (3½ oz) garlic sausage, finely chopped
500 g (1 lb) okra, sliced
1 bay leaf
1 teaspoon thyme
2 teaspoons salt
pepper to taste
pinch of cayenne pepper
2 teaspoons lemon juice
4 cloves
500 g (1 lb) large shelled prawns

TO SERVE
plain boiled rice

1. Heat the butter in a large heavy-based pan. Add the flour and cook, stirring, until lightly browned.

2. Add the onion, pepper, spring onions, parsley and garlic. Cook, stirring, for about 5 minutes, until lightly browned.

3. Add the tomato and garlic sausage and mix thoroughly. Pour in 1.2 litres (2 pints) water, then add the okra, bay leaf, thyme, salt and pepper, cayenne, lemon juice and cloves. Cover and simmer for 20 minutes.

4. Add the prawns and cook for a further 2 minutes to heat through. Stir in a little more water if the mixture is too thick.

5. Serve piping hot in deep bowls, ladled over plain boiled rice.

RIGHT: CREOLE PRAWN GUMBO

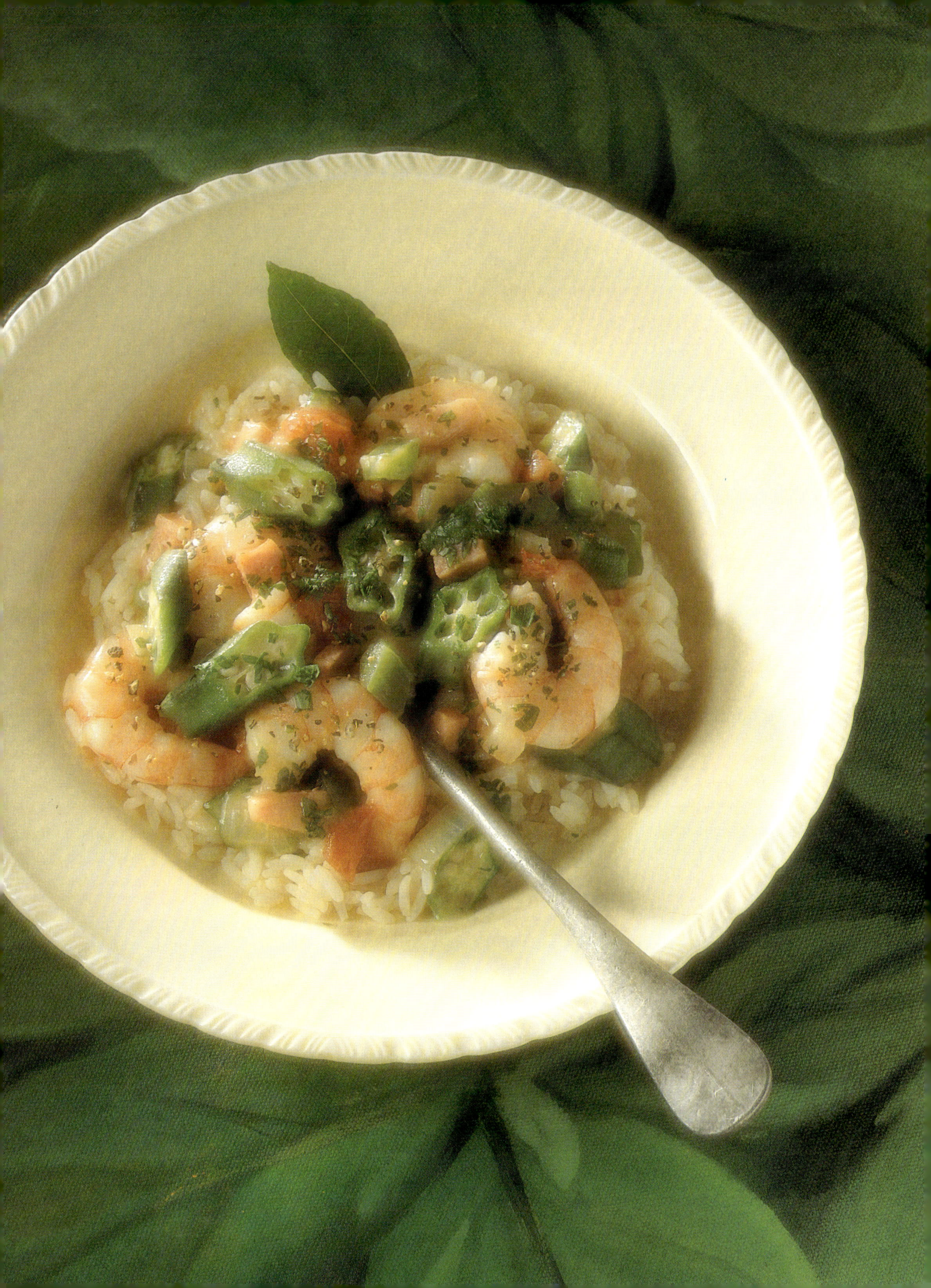

MAIN COURSES

ARTICHOKE RISOTTO

SERVES 4

Short-grained Arborio rice is always used for risotto. It gives a delicious creamy texture.

125 g (4 oz) butter
2 shallots, finely chopped
300 g (10 oz) Arborio rice
5 tablespoons white wine
600 ml (1 pint) vegetable stock
397 g (14 oz) can artichoke hearts, drained and quartered
1 tablespoon chopped chervil
1 tablespoon chopped parsley
25 g (1 oz) freshly grated Parmesan cheese
chervil sprigs to garnish

1. Melt 50 g (2 oz) butter in a pan, add the shallots and fry gently until softened.

2. Add the rice, stirring, until all the grains are coated in butter. Pour in the white wine and bring to the boil. Cook until the volume of liquid is reduced by half.

3. Lower the heat and add a little of the vegetable stock. Stir until the rice has absorbed all the liquid before adding any more. Continue adding liquid in small amounts in this way until the rice is cooked and creamy in texture.

4. Stir in the artichoke hearts, and cook for a few seconds to heat through. Season.

5. Stir in the remaining butter and the Parmesan. Add the chopped herbs and serve immediately, garnished with chervil.

PRAWN & MANGETOUT STIR-FRY

SERVES 4

If raw prawns are unavailable, use defrosted frozen cooked prawns, adding them at the end with the beansprouts, to avoid overcooking.

2 tablespoons vegetable oil
1 clove garlic, finely chopped
1 tablespoon chopped fresh root ginger
250 g (8 oz) raw peeled prawns
125 g (4 oz) mangetout, strings removed
125 g (4 oz) beansprouts
125 ml (4 fl oz) vegetable stock
1 tablespoon red wine vinegar
juice of 1 lime
salt and pepper to taste
lime slices to garnish

1. Heat the oil in a wok or large frying pan. Add the garlic and ginger and stir-fry for about 30 seconds.

2. Add the prawns and stir-fry for 30 seconds, then add the mangetout and cook, stirring, for a further 30 seconds.

3. Add the beansprouts, stock, vinegar and lime juice. Cook over a medium heat until the vegetables are just cooked.

4. Season and serve immediately, garnished with lime slices.

ABOVE: ARTICHOKE RISOTTO *BELOW*: PRAWN & MANGETOUT STIR-FRY

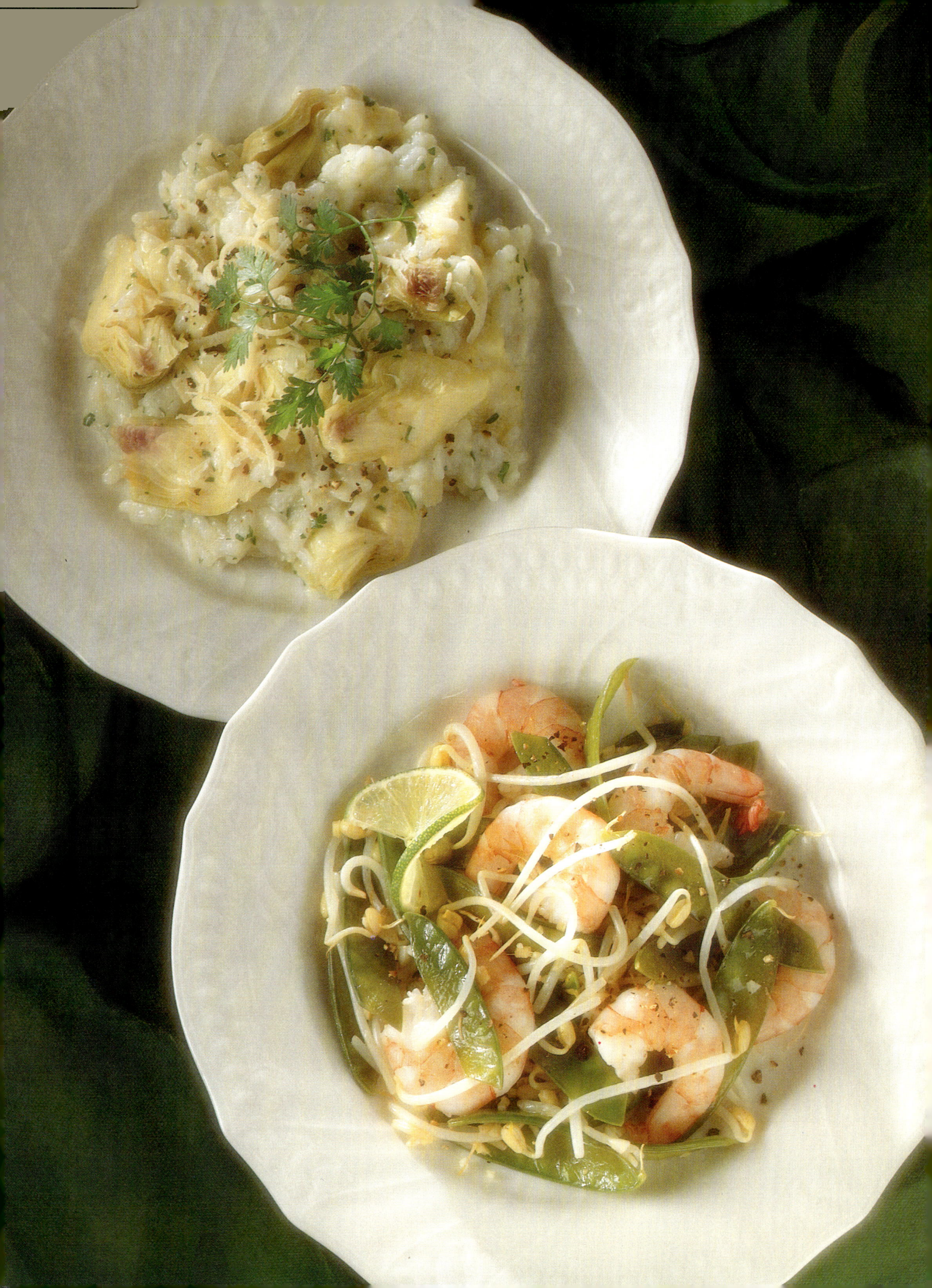

MUSHROOM & CHICKEN GOUGÈRE

SERVES 4

A classic dish from Burgundy in France. The gougère mixture can alternatively be baked in spoonfuls, and eaten as a snack with a glass of wine.

GOUGÈRE
175 ml (6 fl oz) water
65 g (2½ oz) butter
100 g (3½ oz) plain flour, sifted
½ teaspoon salt
3 eggs, beaten
50 g (2 oz) Gruyère or Cheddar cheese, grated

FILLING
25 g (1 oz) butter
1 onion, finely sliced
75 g (3 oz) flat or brown mushrooms, sliced
300 ml (½ pint) ready-to-use béchamel sauce
350 g (12 oz) cooked chicken, diced
1 tablespoon chopped parsley
salt and pepper to taste

TO GARNISH
parsley sprigs

1 Preheat oven to 200°C (400°F/Gas 6).

2 To make the gougère, put the water and butter in a large pan and heat gently until the butter has melted. Bring to the boil, remove from the heat and immediately add the flour and salt, stirring continuously, until the mixture is smooth and leaves the sides of the pan.

3 Gradually beat in the eggs, a little at a time, until the mixture is smooth, shiny and drops fairly easily from the spoon. Stir in the cheese and season with salt and pepper.

4 Spoon the mixture around the edge of a greased 23-25 cm (9-10 inch) gratin dish. Bake for 25-30 minutes, until puffed and golden.

5 To make the filling, melt the butter in a pan, add the onion and cook until softened. Add the mushrooms and cook for 1 minute. Stir in the béchamel sauce, then the chicken and parsley. Simmer for 5 minutes. Season with salt and pepper.

6 Fill the gougère ring with the chicken mixture. Serve cut into wedges and garnished with parsley.

RIGHT: MUSHROOM & CHICKEN GOUGÈRE

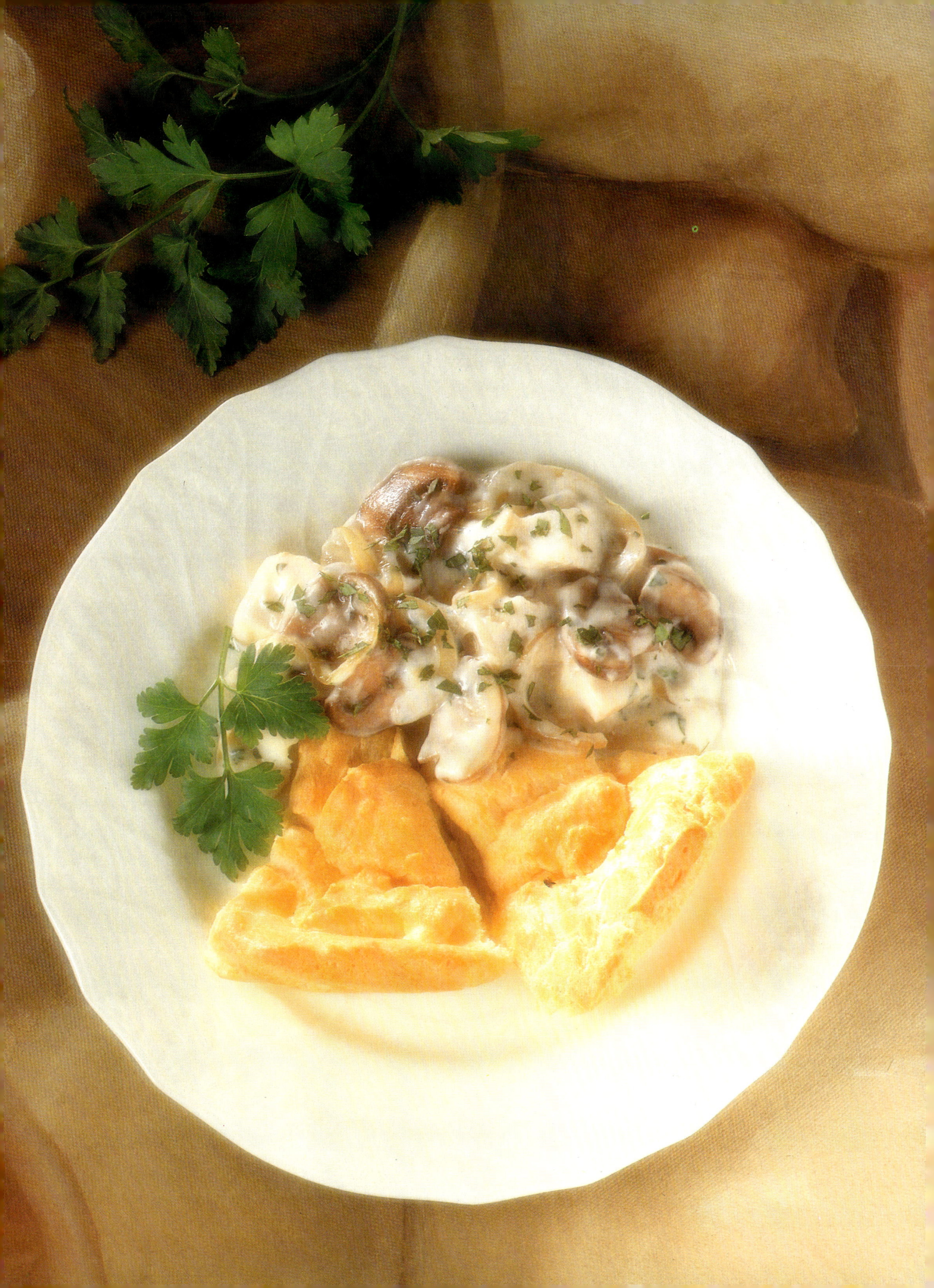

MAIN COURSES

CHILLI BEAN & SAUSAGE CASSEROLE

SERVES 4

A hearty mixture of black eye beans and spicy sausage makes this one-pot dish a perfect supper for a cold winter's night.

2 tablespoons olive oil
1 onion, chopped
2 cloves garlic, crushed
1 small red pepper, cored, seeded and chopped
397 g (14 oz) can chopped tomatoes
1 tablespoon tomato purée
2 tablespoons canned chopped green chillies
1 tablespoon treacle
1 tablespoon dark soft brown sugar
1 bay leaf
salt and pepper to taste
250 g (8 oz) chorizo or other spicy sausage, thickly sliced
435 g (15 oz) can black eye beans, drained
2 tablespoons chopped parsley

1. Heat the oil in a heavy-based pan. Add the onion, garlic and pepper and cook until softened and golden.

2. Add the tomatoes, tomato purée, chillies, treacle, brown sugar, bay leaf and seasoning. Cover and simmer for 15 minutes.

3. Add the chorizo and drained black eye beans, cover and cook for a further 5 minutes. Check the seasoning.

4. Sprinkle with chopped parsley and serve with potatoes or crusty bread.

POT-AU-FEU

SERVES 4-6

Illustrated on back cover.

2 small red onions
8 cloves garlic, unpeeled
4 carrots
1 celery heart
4 small leeks, trimmed
1 bouquet garni
1 cinnamon stick
½ cauliflower, cut into florets
4 large spring onions, trimmed
125 g (4 oz) French beans, trimmed
2 courgettes, quartered lengthwise
125 ml (1¼ pint) white wine
125 g (4 oz) frozen petits pois
4 tomatoes, skinned and quartered
½ teaspoon chilli paste
salt and pepper to taste

1. Simmer the red onions and garlic in boiling water for 20 minutes.

2. Meanwhile, cook the carrots, celery and leeks, with the bouquet garni and cinnamon in sufficient boiling salted water to cover for 5 minutes. Add the cauliflower, spring onions, beans and courgettes and cook for 4 minutes.

3. Drain the onions and garlic, reserving 125 ml (¼ pint) liquid. Peel the garlic and quarter the red onions. Add to the vegetables with the wine, reserved liquor, petit pois, tomatoes, chilli paste and seasoning. Simmer for 2 minutes.

4. Serve with boiled potatoes or rice.

RIGHT: CHILLI BEAN & SAUSAGE CASSEROLE

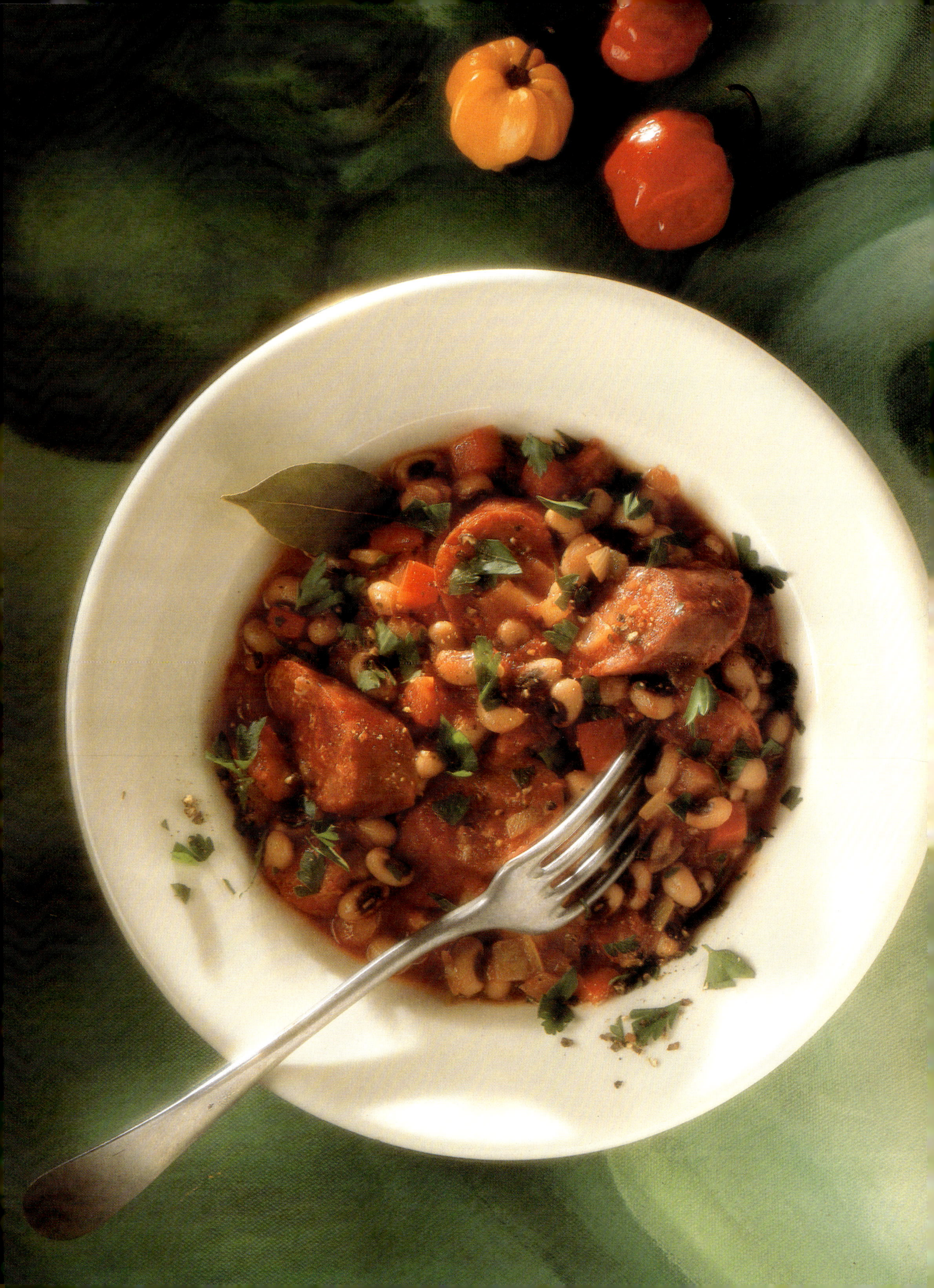

ACCOMPANIMENTS

Accompanying vegetables should be far more adventurous than a spoonful of peas and a few carrots. Recipes needn't be complicated – just a combination of the freshest possible vegetables and a flavoured butter, for example. Simple but delicious. For a special occasion, try little bundles of beans tied with carrot ribbon, or onion and mint purée in toast cups.

Many of these recipes make equally good starters – baby vegetables with herb vinaigrette, for example. Sweet potato and plantain crisps are good nibbles with pre-dinner drinks. Accompaniments deserve to be considered as recipes in their own right.

CONTENTS

GRILLED CHICORY & RADICCHIO	64
BABY VEGETABLES WITH HERB VINAIGRETTE	64
STIR-FRIED CHARD WITH GARLIC	66
SWEET POTATO & PLANTAIN CRISPS	66
SAUTÉED CARROT & COURGETTE	68
SWEET & SOUR PEPPER 'NOODLES'	68
STIR-FRIED SPICY CUCUMBER	70
STIR-FRIED BROCCOLI WITH HOISIN SAUCE	70
SAUTÉED CHERRY TOMATOES	72
SUGAR SNAPS WITH CHILLI BUTTER	72
CARROT RIBBONS WITH MUSTARD SEEDS	74
FRENCH BEAN BUNDLES	74
MINTED ONION IN TOAST 'CUPS'	76
ROAST VEGETABLES WITH GREMOLATA	76
BROAD BEANS WITH MUSHROOMS & BACON	78
GLAZED RADISHES	78
BABY BEETS WITH FROMAGE FRAIS	80
PEAS WITH RADICCHIO	80
SPINACH & RICE PILAF	82
CORN & PIMIENTO FRITTERS	82

ACCOMPANIMENTS

GRILLED RADICCHIO & CHICORY

SERVES 4

This dish is an excellent accompaniment to grilled meat. It also works well cooked on the barbecue.

4 large spring onions
250 g (8 oz) chicory
250 g (8 oz) radicchio
4 garlic cloves, unpeeled
5 tablespoons quality olive oil
salt and pepper to taste
125 g (4 oz) piece Parmesan cheese

1. Preheat grill to medium.

2. Halve the spring onions lengthwise. Cut the chicory and radicchio into quarters lengthwise. Place the radicchio, chicory, spring onions and garlic in the grill pan. Pour over the olive oil and season with salt and pepper.

3. Grill the vegetables for about 10 minutes until lightly browned.

4. Using a potato peeler, pare the Parmesan cheese into shavings. Transfer the vegetables to a serving dish and top with the Parmesan.

BABY VEGETABLES WITH HERB VINAIGRETTE

SERVES 4

This attractive accompaniment can be prepared and cooked in less than 10 minutes. It is equally delicious served warm or cold. Vary the choice of vegetables according to availability, or use larger varieties cut into chunks.

125 g (4 oz) baby carrots
125 g (4 oz) baby cauliflower, quartered
125 g (4 oz) baby patty pan squashes or courgettes
125 g (4 oz) sprue asparagus
salt and pepper to taste

VINAIGRETTE
90 ml (3 fl oz) olive oil
2 tablespoons white wine vinegar
1 teaspoon tarragon mustard
1 tablespoon chopped tarragon

1. Bring a large pan of salted water to the boil. Add the carrots, cauliflower and patty pans or courgettes and cook for 2 minutes. Add the asparagus and cook for 2 minutes; drain. If serving cold, plunge the vegetables into cold water to cool quickly; drain.

2. Whisk together the ingredients for the vinaigrette with salt and pepper to taste in a bowl until thoroughly combined.

3. Arrange the vegetables on individual serving plates and pour over the vinaigrette to serve.

ABOVE: GRILLED RADICCHIO & CHICORY   BELOW: BABY VEGETABLES WITH HERB VINAIGRETTE

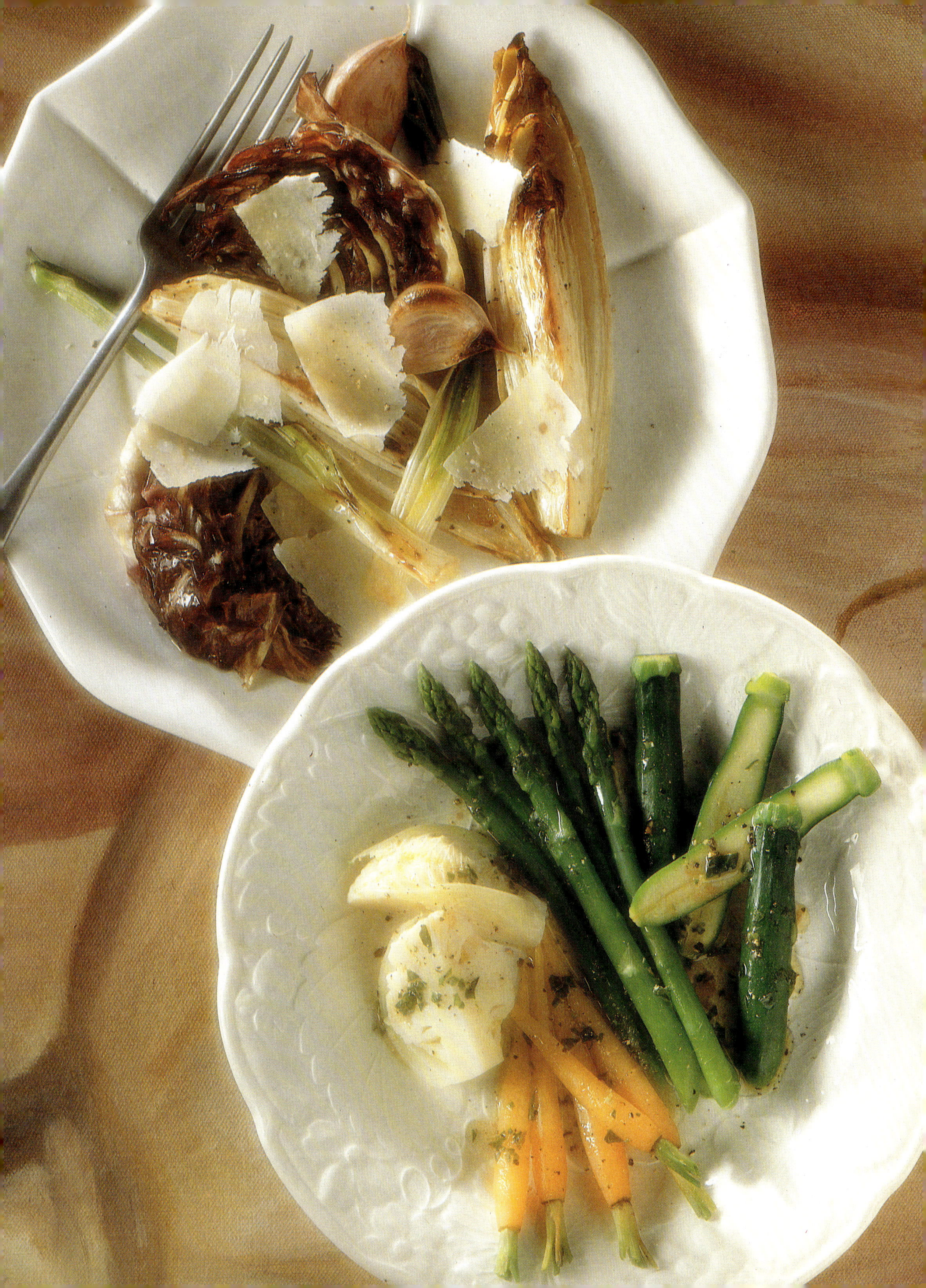

ACCOMPANIMENTS

STIR-FRIED CHARD WITH GARLIC

SERVES 4

This recipe only uses the leaves of the vegetable, but if you've chosen young chard, you will find the stems are delicious steamed and served with melted butter.

750 g (1½ lb) Swiss chard
3 tablespoons olive oil
6 cloves garlic, finely chopped
2 tablespoons balsamic or sherry vinegar
salt and pepper to taste

1. Remove the stalks from the chard and roughly chop the leaves.

2. Heat the olive oil in a large frying pan or wok. Add the garlic and cook, stirring, for about 30 seconds.

3. Add the chard and stir-fry over a high heat until limp. (You may need to cook in two batches because of the bulk.)

4. Add the vinegar, season with salt and pepper and toss well. Serve hot or cold.

SWEET POTATO & PLANTAIN CRISPS

SERVES 4

When choosing plantains, look for black ones as this indicates ripeness – unlike bananas! Alternatively, buy them green and ripen on a sunny windowsill.

vegetable oil for deep-frying
1 ripe plantain, peeled and thinly sliced
1 orange-fleshed sweet potato, peeled and thinly sliced
coarse sea salt to taste

1. Half-fill a deep-fryer with oil and heat to 190°C (375°F).

2. Immerse the sliced plantain and sweet potato in a large bowl of cold water. Swirl around, drain and dry thoroughly on kitchen paper.

3. Deep-fry the plantain and sweet potato in small batches in the hot oil for about 2 minutes, until browned. Drain on kitchen paper.

4. Sprinkle with salt to serve.

ABOVE: STIR-FRIED CHARD WITH GARLIC *BELOW*: SWEET POTATO & PLANTAIN CRISPS

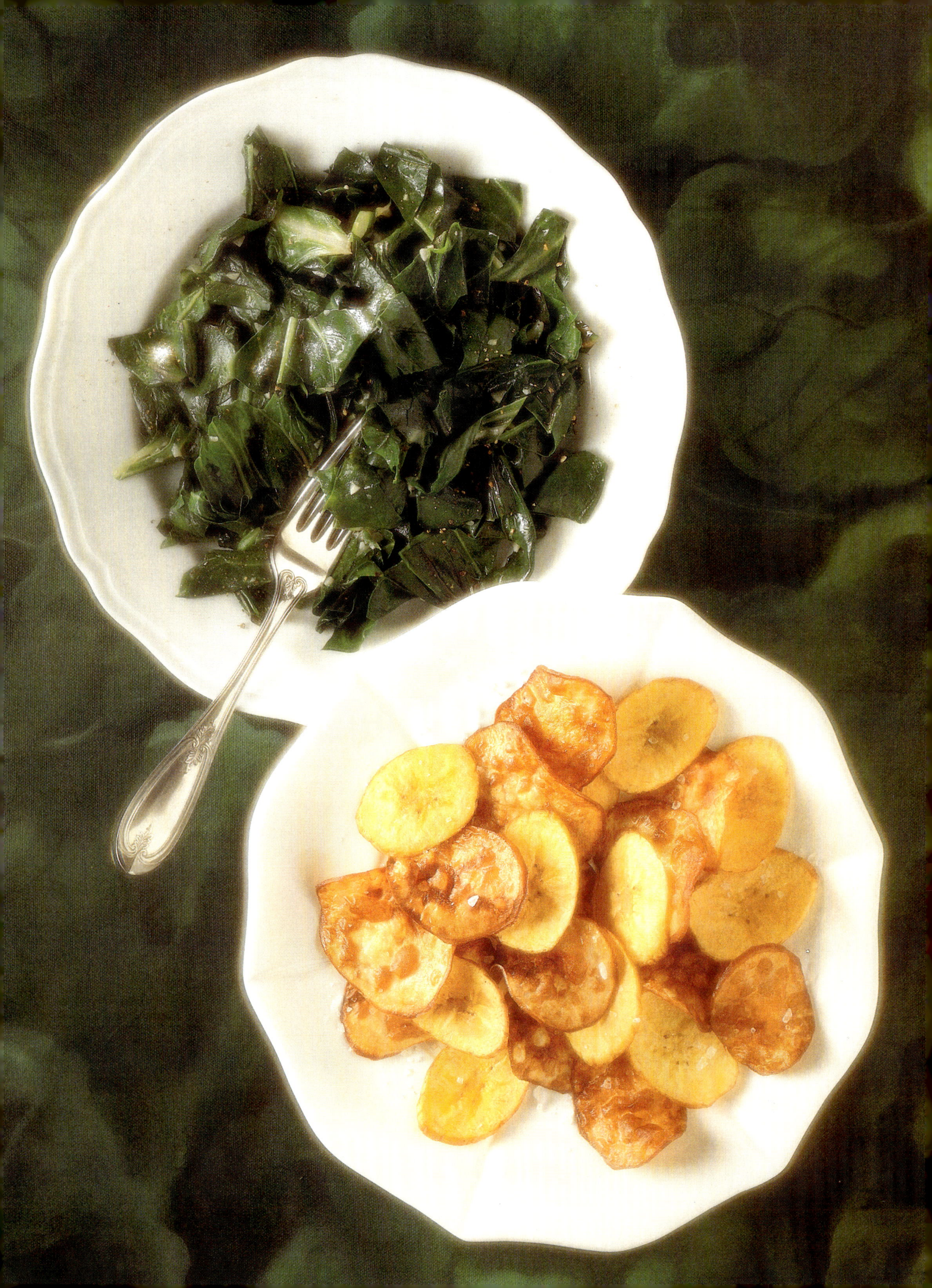

SAUTÉED CARROT & COURGETTE

SERVES 4

An exceptionally quick accompaniment. The vegetables are very finely grated, so they cook quickly. Try this method with other root vegetables too, such as celeriac, beetroot and parsnips.

50 g (2 oz) butter
350 g (12 oz) carrots, finely grated
350 g (12 oz) courgettes, finely grated
salt and pepper to taste
parsley sprigs to garnish

1. Heat the butter in a sauté pan until foaming. When the foaming subsides, add the carrots and courgettes and sauté for 3-4 minutes, until almost all the liquid has evaporated.

2. Season with salt and pepper. Serve immediately, garnished with parsley.

SWEET & SOUR PEPPER 'NOODLES'

SERVES 4

Use the longest peppers you can find for this dish and cut them as finely as possible.

50 g (2 oz) tagliatelle or thin noodles
1 large red pepper
1 large green pepper
1 large yellow pepper
1 tablespoon olive oil
1 tablespoon white wine vinegar
1 tablespoon sugar
salt and pepper to taste

1. Cook the pasta in boiling salted water for about 10 minutes until just tender.

2. Meanwhile cut the peppers into long fine strips, discarding the core and seeds. Heat the olive oil in a sauté pan, add the peppers and sauté until softened.

3. Add the vinegar, allow to bubble for a few seconds, then add the sugar. Cook, stirring, for a few seconds longer.

4. Drain the pasta thoroughly and mix with the pepper 'noodles'. Season with salt and pepper.

5. Arrange in 'nests' on individual serving plates by twisting the 'noodles' around a fork. Serve immediately.

ABOVE: SAUTÉED CARROT & COURGETTE *BELOW*: SWEET & SOUR PEPPER 'NOODLES'

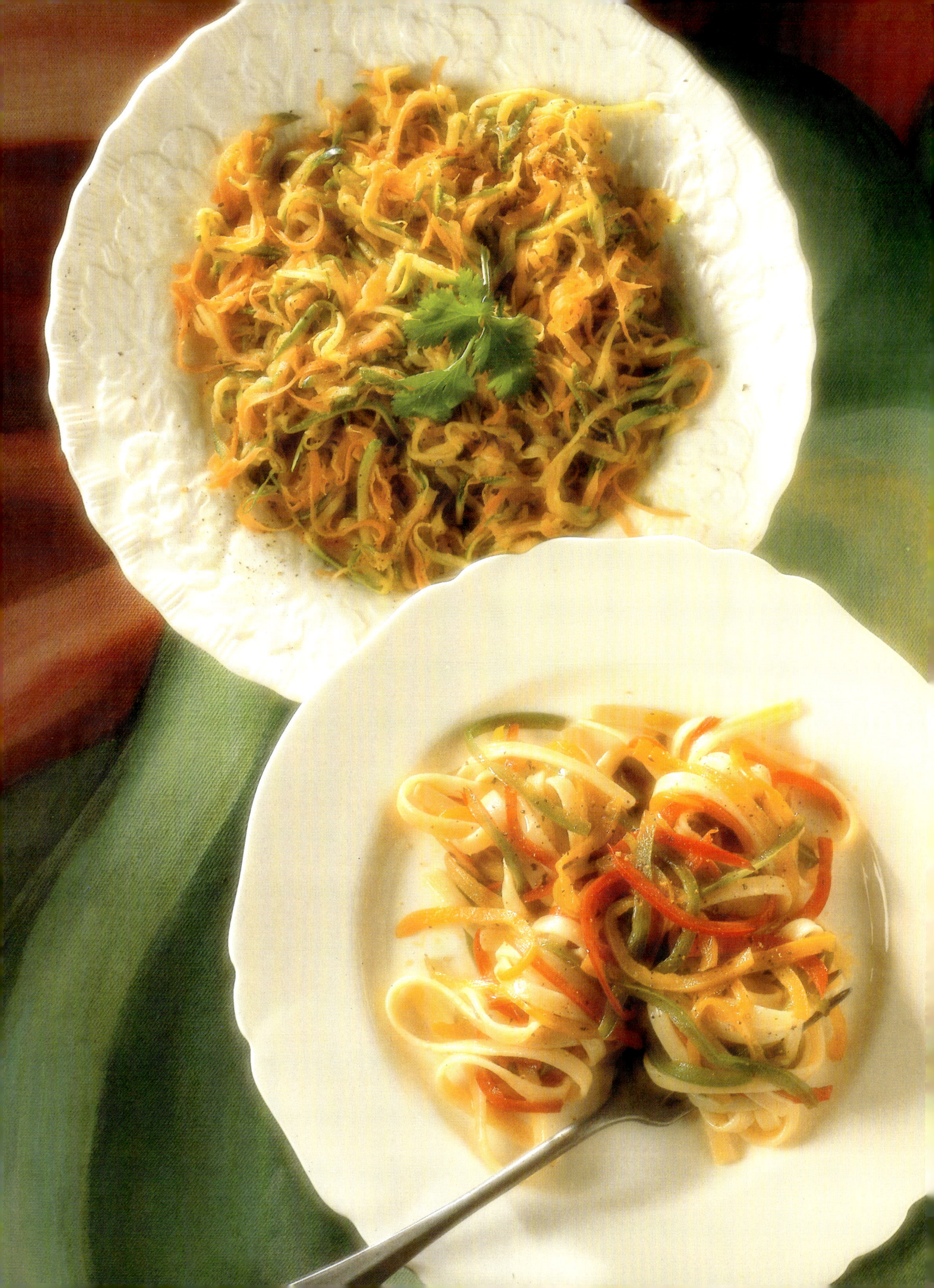

STIR-FRIED SPICY CUCUMBER

SERVES 4-6

Although we usually eat cucumber raw, it is delicious cooked and makes a good accompaniment to fish. Canned salted black beans are available from Chinese food stores.

750 g (1½ lb) cucumbers
2 teaspoons salt
1 tablespoon oil
¼ teaspoon chilli powder
1 clove garlic, finely chopped
1½ tablespoons salted black beans
1 teaspoon sesame oil
parsley sprigs to garnish

1. Using a canelle knife, cut thin grooves along the cucumber if you wish.

2. Halve the cucumbers lengthwise and scoop out the seeds with a teaspoon. Cut the flesh into 2.5 cm (1 inch) cubes. Sprinkle with the salt and leave to drain in a colander for 15-20 minutes. Rinse and dry with kitchen paper.

3. Heat the oil in a wok or frying pan. Add the chilli powder, garlic and black beans. Cook, stirring, for 30 seconds.

4. Add the cucumber, stir well, then pour in 125 ml (4 fl oz) water. Stir-fry over a high heat for 3-4 minutes, until most of the water has evaporated.

5. Add the sesame oil and serve immediately, garnished with parsley.

STIR-FRIED BROCCOLI WITH HOISIN SAUCE

SERVES 4

Hoisin sauce is made from soy beans, flavoured with garlic and chilli. Also known as barbecue sauce, it can be found in most large supermarkets.

500 g (1 lb) broccoli florets
1 tablespoon oil
1 clove garlic, finely chopped
2 tablespoons hoisin sauce
2 teaspoons sesame seeds

1. Cook the broccoli in boiling salted water for about 5 minutes, until just tender. Drain, then plunge into cold water to preserve the colour. Drain thoroughly.

2. Heat the oil in a large frying pan or wok, add the broccoli and garlic and stir-fry for about 1 minute. Add the hoisin sauce and 3 tablespoons water and stir-fry for 5 minutes.

3. Add the sesame seeds, toss well and serve immediately.

ABOVE: STIR-FRIED SPICY CUCUMBER   BELOW: STIR-FRIED BROCCOLI WITH HOISIN SAUCE

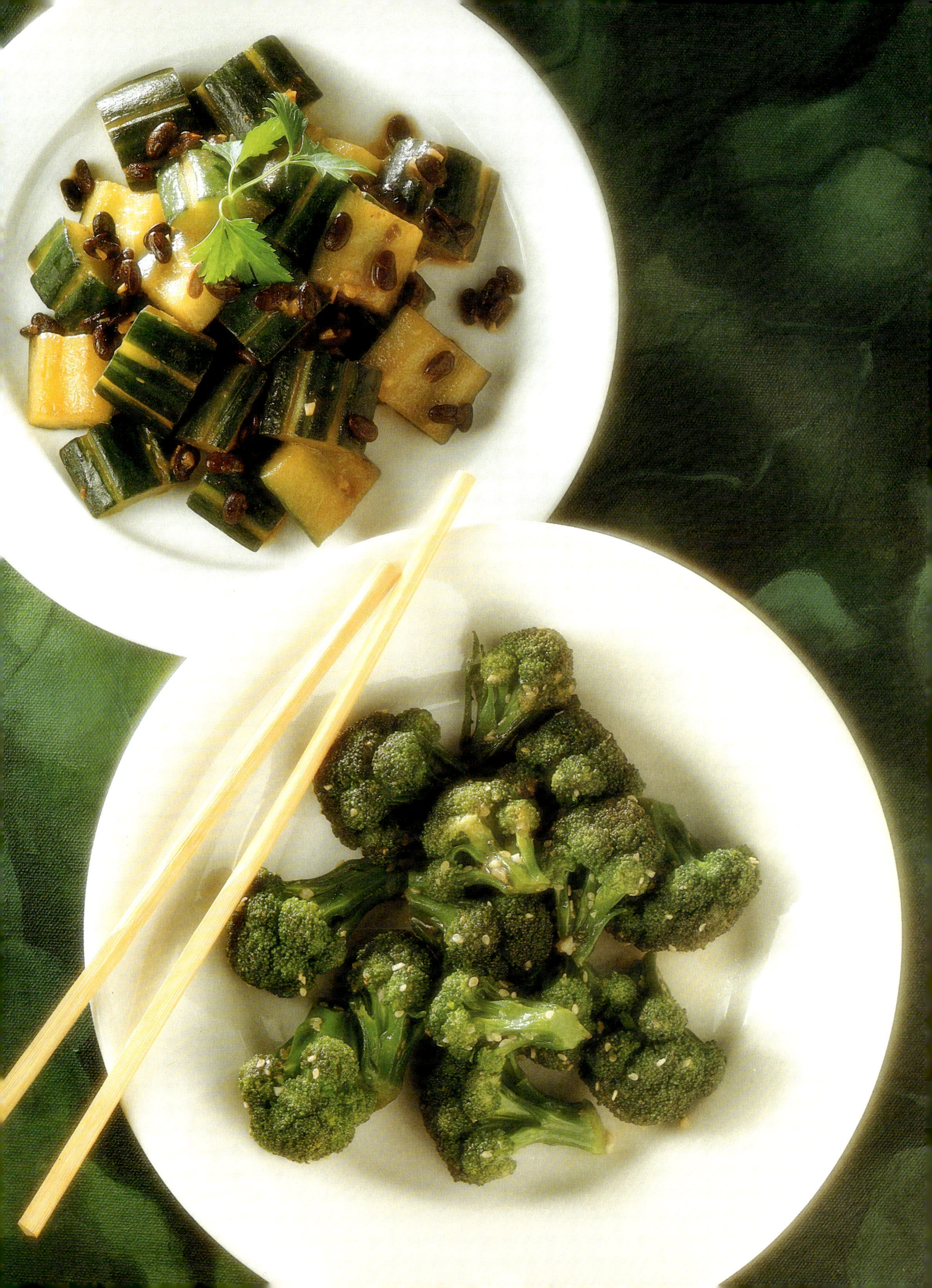

ACCOMPANIMENTS

SAUTÉED CHERRY TOMATOES WITH HERBS

SERVES 4

Don't confine cherry tomatoes to salads – cooked in this way, they make a delicious accompaniment to grilled meats. If the yellow variety is available, use a mixture of the two colours.

40 g (1½ oz) butter
1 small red onion, finely sliced
2 spring onions, sliced
1 teaspoon dill
1 teaspoon chopped parsley
275 g (9 oz) cherry tomatoes
salt and pepper to taste
parsley sprigs to garnish

1. Melt the butter in a sauté pan. Add the red onion, spring onions, dill and parsley. Cook gently, stirring, for 5 minutes.

2. Add the cherry tomatoes and sauté for 5 minutes, until their skins are beginning to split. Season with salt and pepper.

3. Serve immediately, garnished with parsley sprigs.

SUGAR SNAPS WITH COCONUT & CHILLI BUTTER

SERVES 4

The tasty flavoured butter in this recipe can be used with a variety of vegetables – try it with French beans, broccoli, baby corn, or a mixture of these.

50 g (2 oz) butter, softened
1 small red chilli, seeded and finely chopped
1 spring onion, finely chopped
grated rind of ½ lime
25 g (1 oz) creamed coconut
350 g (12 oz) sugar snaps, strings removed

1. Melt 15 g (½ oz) of the butter in a small pan. Add the chilli and spring onion and cook until softened. Add the lime rind and creamed coconut, stirring until the coconut has dissolved. Remove from the heat.

2. Leave to cool for about 10 minutes, then beat into the remaining butter. Pack into a small bowl and place in the freezer for 5 minutes.

3. Cook the sugar snaps in boiling salted water for 5 minutes; drain.

4. Using a melon baller, scoop the flavoured butter into balls.

5. Place the sugar snaps in a warmed serving dish and dot with the butter balls. Serve immediately.

ABOVE: SAUTÉED CHERRY TOMATOES WITH HERBS *BELOW:* SUGAR SNAPS WITH COCONUT & CHILLI BUTTER

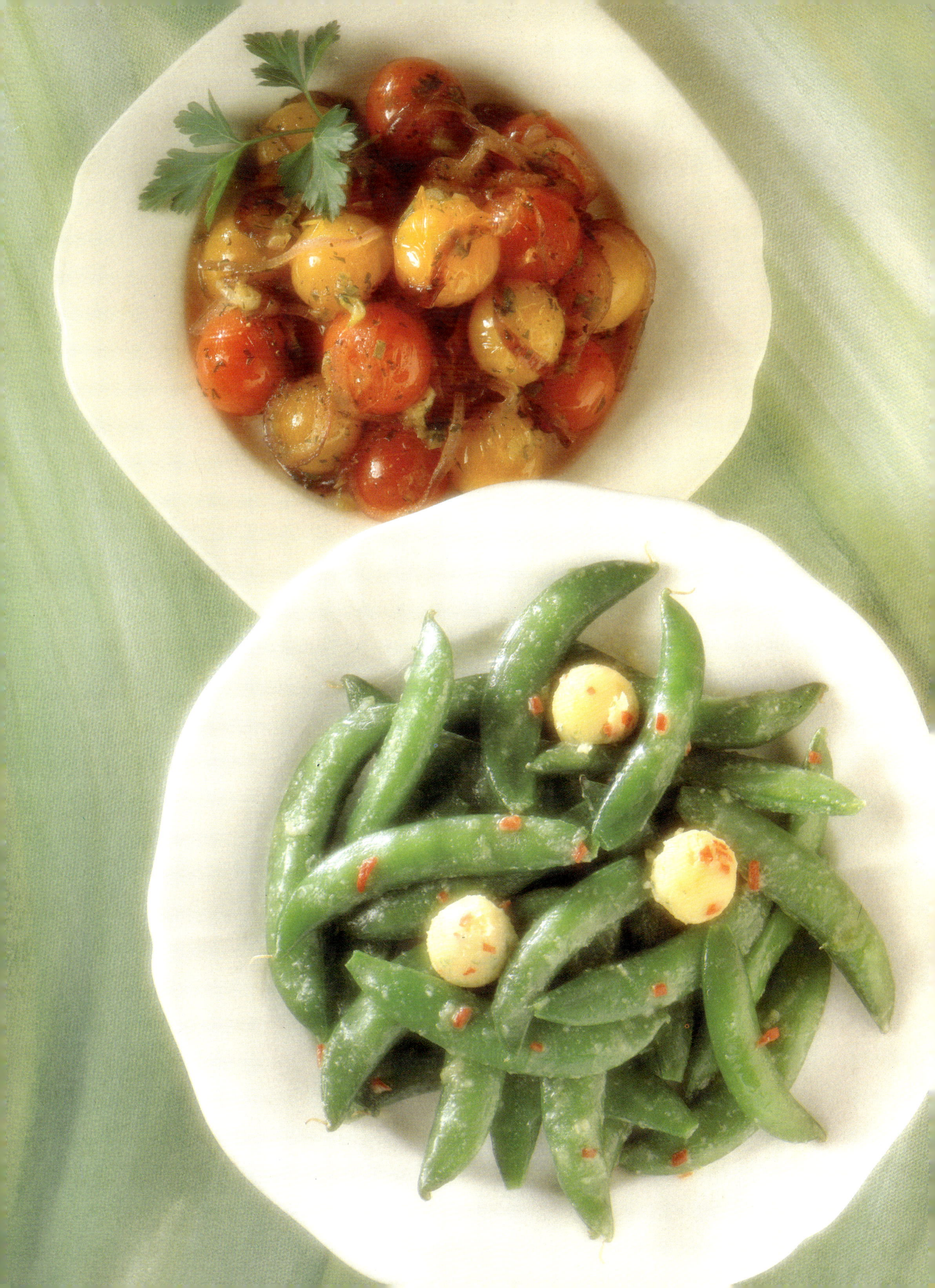

ACCOMPANIMENTS

CARROT RIBBONS WITH MUSTARD SEEDS

SERVES 4

Black mustard seeds impart their flavour when heated in oil. You can use poppy seeds instead, but don't heat them.

500 g (1 lb) carrots
1 tablespoon vegetable oil
1 teaspoon black mustard seeds
1 tablespoon sesame oil
parsley or chervil sprigs to garnish

1. Using a potato peeler, pare long ribbons along the length of each carrot. Prepare as many ribbons as possible, dropping them into a bowl of iced water as you do so to enable them to curl.

2. Drain, then place in a steamer basket or sieve over a pan of boiling water. Steam, covered, for 8-10 minutes until tender, but retaining a slight crunch.

3. Heat the vegetable oil in a small pan, add the black mustard seeds and continue to heat until the seeds start to pop. Immediately pour over the carrot ribbons. Add sesame oil and toss well.

4. Serve hot or cold, garnished with parsley or chervil.

FRENCH BEAN BUNDLES

SERVES 4

A pretty way of serving beans – perfect for a smart dinner party. As an alternative, serve cold tossed in vinaigrette with a platter of cold meats.

250 g (8 oz) French beans, trimmed
1 long carrot
25 g (1 oz) melted butter
few thyme sprigs

1. Divide the French beans into 4 equal portions.

2. Using a potato peeler, pare 4 long strips of carrot. Lay each one flat and place a bundle of beans on top. Carefully tie the carrot ribbon around the beans.

3. Transfer the bean bundles to a steaming basket or sieve over a pan of boiling water. Steam, covered, for 10 minutes.

4. Using a spatula, gently lift the bundles out and place on a serving dish. Drizzle with melted butter, garnish with thyme and serve immediately.

ABOVE: CARROT RIBBONS WITH MUSTARD SEEDS   *BELOW*: FRENCH BEAN BUNDLES

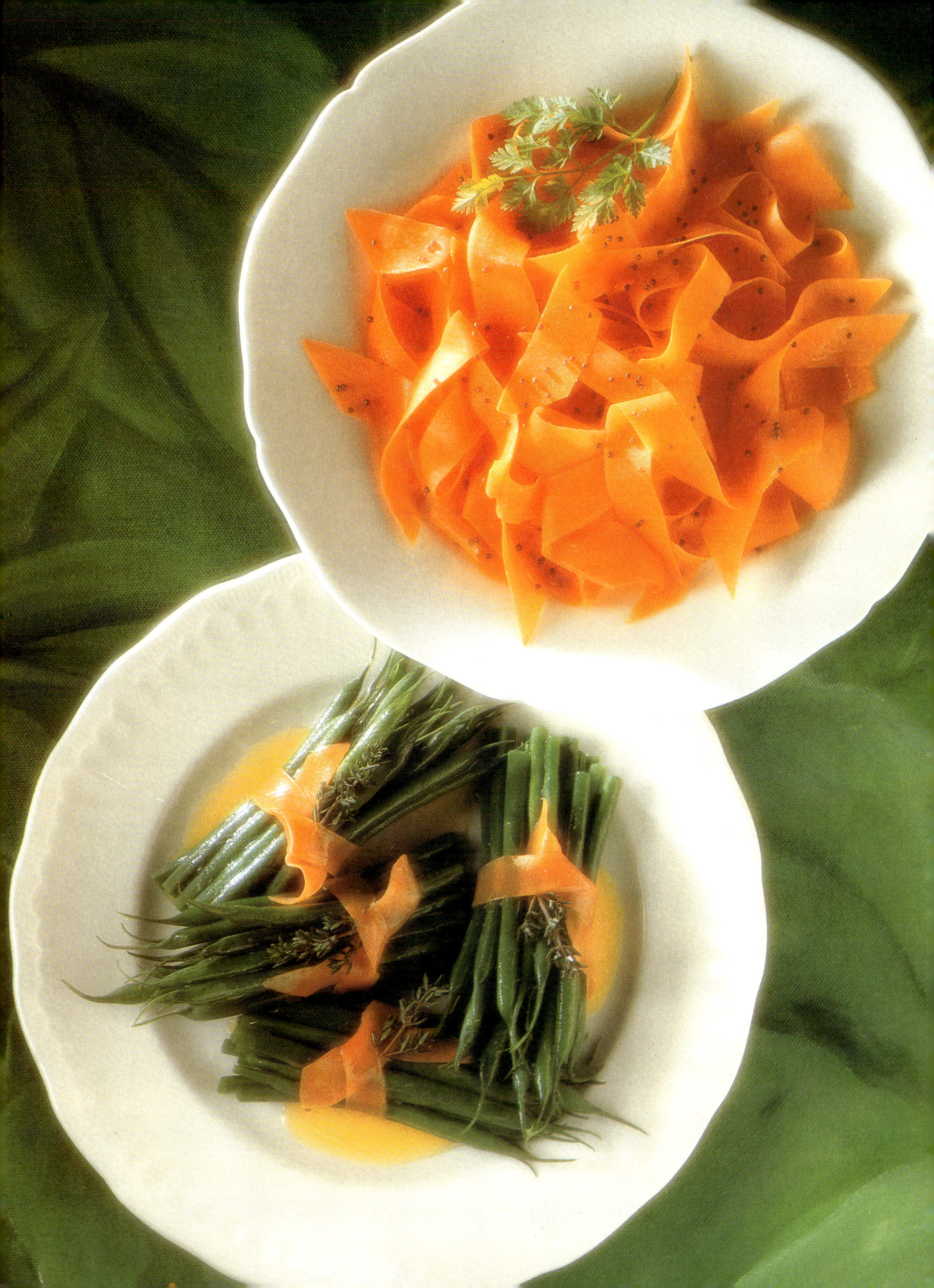

MINTED ONION IN TOAST CUPS

SERVES 6

These little tarts make a smart accompaniment to roast lamb.

6 slices of white bread
75 g (3 oz) butter
1 large onion, finely chopped
2 tablespoons chopped mint
salt and pepper to taste
mint leaves to garnish

1. Preheat oven to 200°C (400°F/Gas 6).

2. Remove the crusts from the bread and cut a 6 cm (2½ inch) square from each slice. Flatten each one with a rolling pin.

3. Melt 25 g (1 oz) of the butter and use to brush both sides of the bread squares. Line 6 tartlet tins with the bread squares, pressing in firmly. Bake for 10-12 minutes, until golden.

4. Meanwhile, melt the remaining butter with 3 tablespoons water. Add the onion and cook gently, covered, for about 10 minutes until softened. Transfer to a food processor, add the mint and work to a purée. Season with salt and pepper.

5. Fill the toast cups with the onion and mint purée. Garnish with mint leaves to serve.

ROAST VEGETABLES WITH GREMOLATA

SERVES 4

Gremolata is an Italian mixture of flat-leaved parsley, garlic and lemon rind. It gives these vegetables a delicious flavour. Use flat-leaved parsley rather than the curly variety if possible.

125 g (4 oz) small new potatoes
1 red pepper, quartered lengthwise and seeded
1 aubergine, thickly sliced
2 courgettes, halved lengthwise
4 tablespoons olive oil
1 tablespoon coarse sea salt
pepper to taste

GREMOLATA
2 cloves garlic
grated rind of 1 lemon
2 tablespoons chopped parsley

1. Preheat oven to 200°C (400°F/Gas 6).

2. Place all the vegetables in a roasting tin. Pour over the olive oil and sprinkle with the sea salt. Roast in the oven for 30 minutes, basting occasionally with the oil, until tender and lightly browned.

3. For the gremolata, mix together the garlic, lemon rind and parsley.

4. Transfer the vegetables to a warmed serving dish, season with pepper and sprinkle with the gremolata.

ABOVE: MINTED ONION IN TOAST CUPS   *BELOW*: ROAST VEGETABLES WITH GREMOLATA

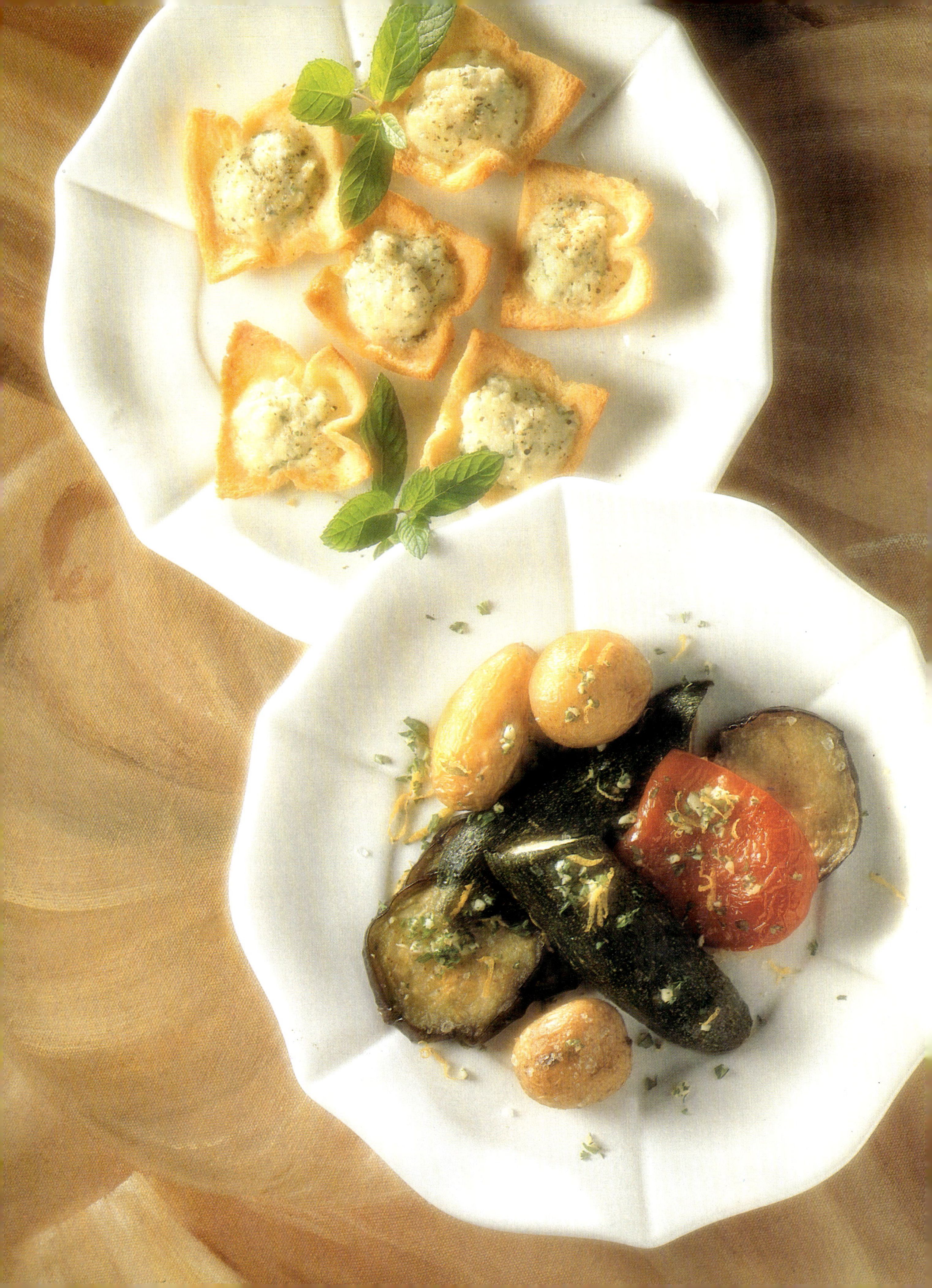

BROAD BEANS WITH MUSHROOMS & BACON

SERVES 4

You can use frozen broad beans if fresh ones are out of season. If they are large, it's worth peeling them – the skins can be tough, and they're a very pretty green underneath.

250 g (8 oz) broad beans
4 rashers streaky bacon, derinded
4 tablespoons olive oil
250 g (8 oz) button mushrooms, halved
salt and pepper to taste
1 tablespoon chopped chives
parsley sprigs to garnish

1. Cook the broad beans in boiling salted water for 7-8 minutes. Drain and plunge into cold water. Peel, if necessary.

2. Cut the bacon into strips. Heat the oil in a sauté pan, add the bacon and mushrooms and cook for 2 minutes. Add the broad beans and cook, stirring, for 2 minutes until heated through. Season with salt and pepper.

3. Transfer to a serving dish and sprinkle with chives. Garnish with parsley to serve.

GLAZED RADISHES

SERVES 4

We usually think of eating radishes raw, but cooking them in this way gives a mellow flavour and turns them a delicate pink colour. Serve with roast meats and game.

2 bunches of radishes, trimmed, about 325 g
   (11 oz) trimmed weight
15 g (½ oz) butter
1 teaspoon sugar
salt and pepper to taste
chervil or parsley sprigs to garnish

1. Put the radishes, butter and sugar into a sauté pan or deep frying pan. Add just enough water to cover and season with salt and pepper.

2. Bring to the boil and simmer, uncovered, for 10 minutes, shaking the pan occasionally, until the water has evaporated. The radishes will become a pinky-purple colour, and have a slight glaze.

3. Serve immediately, garnished with chervil or parsley.

ABOVE: BROAD BEANS WITH MUSHROOMS & BACON *BELOW*: GLAZED RADISHES

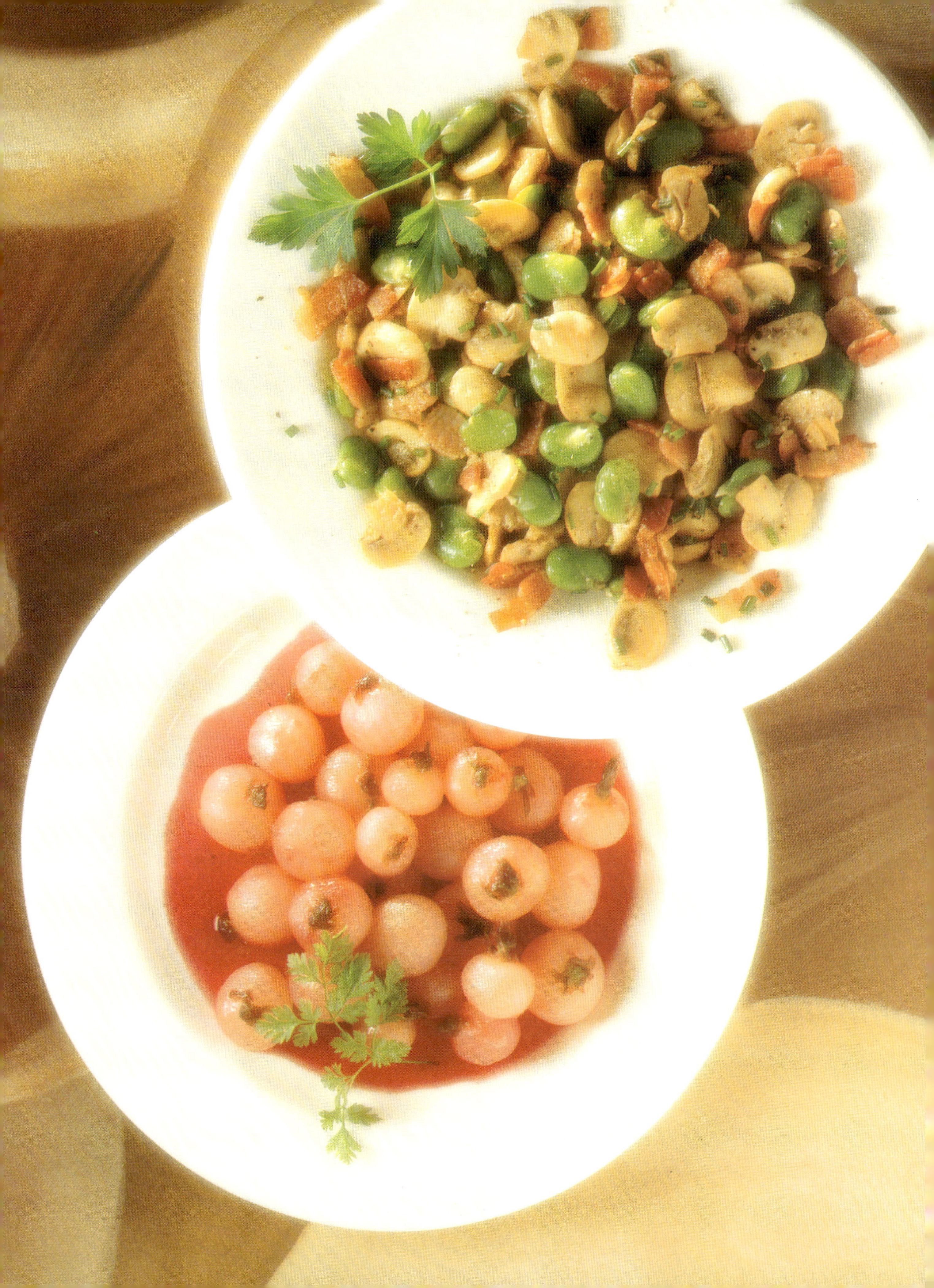

BABY BEETS WITH FROMAGE FRAIS

SERVES 4

Steaming is a quick, but gentle method of cooking, retaining more of the vitamin C in vegetables than boiling. It's also a good way of reheating cooked foods, without destroying their shape and texture.

325 g (11 oz) cooked baby beetroot
125 ml (4 fl oz) fromage frais
1 tablespoon chopped dill
salt and pepper to taste
dill sprigs to garnish

1. Using a sharp knife, slice the beetroot at 2.5 cm (1 inch) intervals, leaving about 5 mm (¼ inch) intact at the base, to prevent them falling apart.

2. Place the beetroot in a heatproof dish which will fit inside a steaming basket or sieve, gently fanning them into position.

3. Place in the basket or sieve, cover and steam over boiling water for 8-10 minutes.

4. Mix the fromage frais with the chopped dill and seasoning.

5. Lift the beetroot out of the steamer and drain off any excess liquid. Arrange on a serving dish and spoon over the fromage frais. Serve immediately, garnished with dill.

PEAS WITH RADICCHIO

SERVES 4

Use frozen peas if fresh ones are not available. Young peas are the most successful – their sweetness complements the slightly bitter flavour of radicchio perfectly.

500 g (1 lb) shelled peas
mint sprig
salt and pepper to taste
25 g (1 oz) butter
125 g (4 oz) radicchio, finely shredded
mint sprigs to garnish

1. Put the peas in a saucepan containing about 1 cm (½ inch) depth of water. Add the mint and seasoning. Bring to the boil, cover and simmer gently for about 5 minutes, until the peas are tender.

2. Remove the mint and drain off the liquid from the peas. Add the butter and return to the heat. When the butter has melted, add the radicchio. Cook for a few seconds until the radicchio is warmed through, but retains its colour.

3. Serve immediately, garnished with mint.

ABOVE: BABY BEETS WITH FROMAGE FRAIS *BELOW*: PEAS WITH RADICCHIO

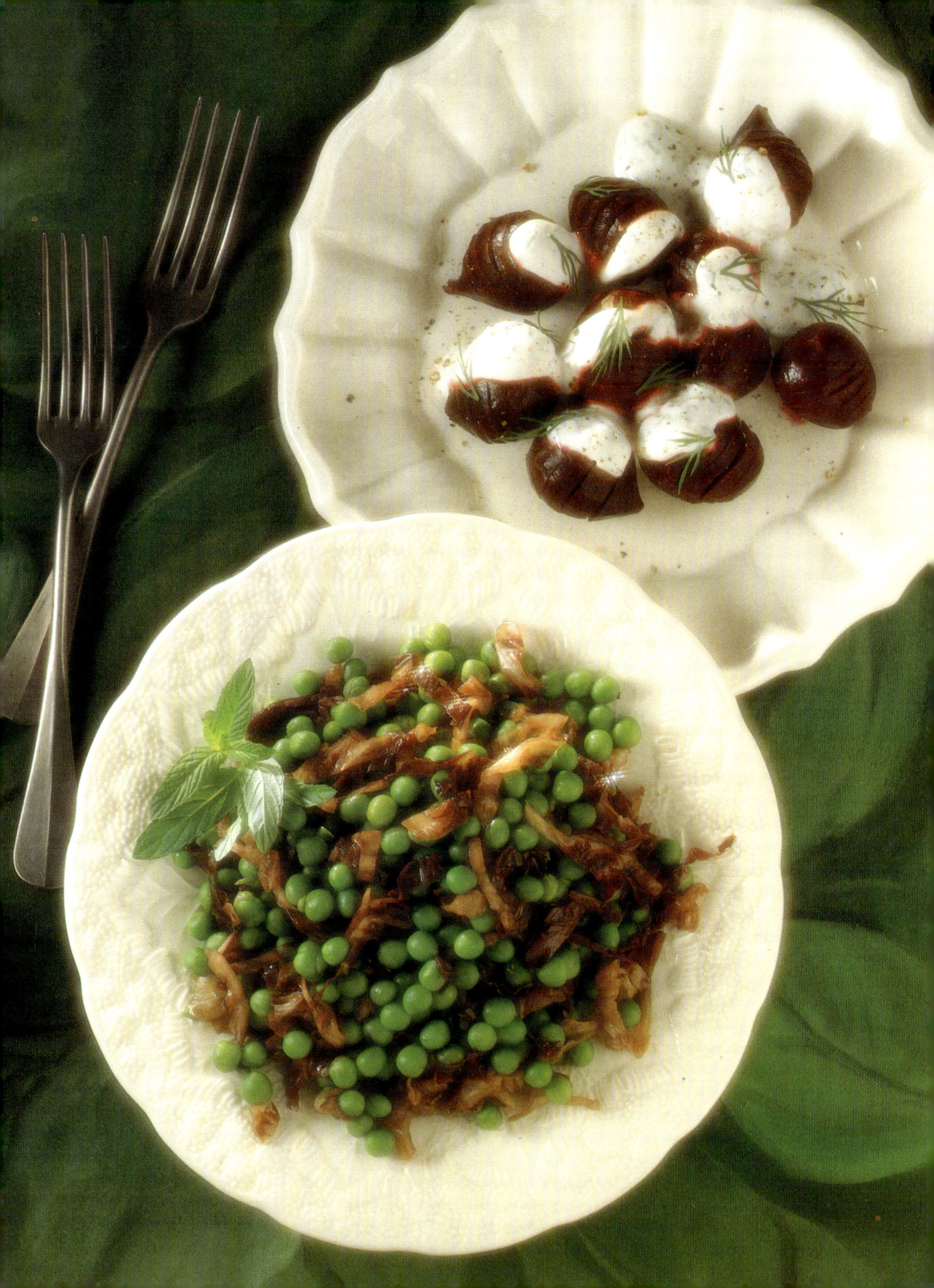

SPINACH RICE PILAF

SERVES 6

This pilaf makes a perfect accompaniment to Indian dishes, such as curries or other spiced foods. Turn it into a meal in itself by adding cooked chopped chicken or prawns, 5 minutes before the end of cooking.

350 g (12 oz) basmati rice
2 tablespoons vegetable oil
1 large onion, finely chopped
350 g (12 oz) frozen chopped spinach, defrosted and squeezed dry
50 g (2 oz) raisins
50 g (2 oz) unsalted cashew nuts, roughly chopped
juice of ½ lemon
salt and pepper to taste
chervil or parsley sprigs to garnish

1. Wash and rinse the basmati rice several times to remove the starch.

2. Heat the oil in a heavy-based pan, add the onion and cook until softened. Add the rice and cook, stirring, until translucent.

3. Add the spinach, raisins and nuts, then stir in 450 ml (¾ pint) water. Bring to the boil, cover and simmer until the water is absorbed and the rice is fluffy. Top up with more water if necessary, during cooking.

4. Add the lemon juice and seasoning. Garnish with chervil or parsley to serve.

CORN & PIMIENTO FRITTERS

SERVES 6

These American-style fritters are traditionally served with fried chicken.

140 g (4½ oz) plain flour
pinch of salt
2 eggs, 1 separated
225-275 ml (8-10 fl oz) milk
1 tablespoon oil
vegetable oil for shallow-frying
283 g (10 oz) can sweetcorn, drained
½ small red pepper, cored, seeded and finely chopped
salt and pepper to taste
parsley sprigs to garnish

1. Sift the flour and salt into a large mixing bowl and make a well in the centre. Add 1 whole egg, plus 1 egg yolk. Mix to a smooth paste.

2. Gradually add the milk and beat until creamy. Stir in the oil.

3. Heat the vegetable oil in a deep frying pan to 190°C (375°F).

4. Whisk the egg white until stiff, then fold into the batter. Fold in the sweetcorn, red pepper and seasoning.

5. Drop large spoonfuls of the mixture into the hot oil and fry for 2 minutes on each side, until puffed and golden.

6. Drain on kitchen paper and serve immediately, garnished with parsley.

ABOVE: SPINACH RICE PILAF BELOW: CORN & PIMIENTO FRITTERS

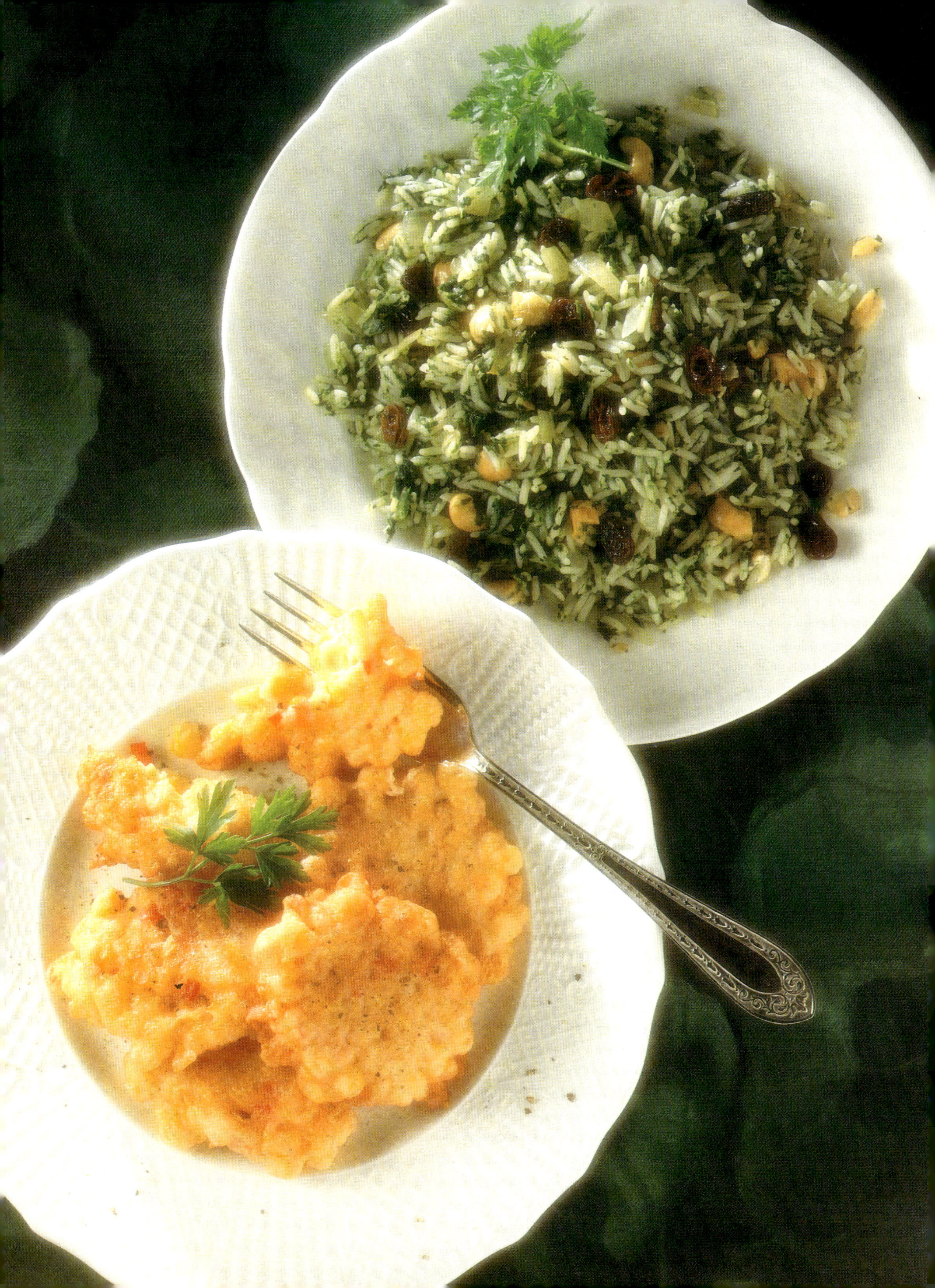

SNACKS

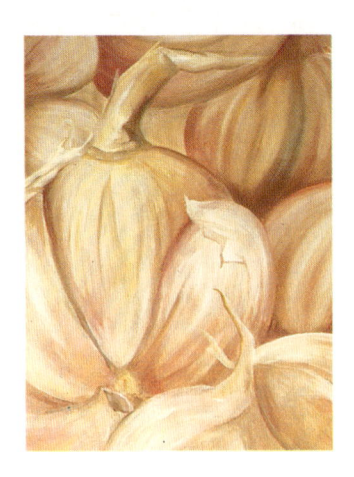

Vegetables are perfect snack food eaten just as they are. Crunchy carrots, celery sticks and cherry tomatoes all make quick, nutritious nibbles. With a minimum of effort, vegetables can be transformed into more imaginative snacks. Baked potatoes can be served with a variety of delicious fillings. Tortilla chips topped with vegetables make irresistible speedy mouthfuls.

Many of the ideas here can be served as party food if made in mini portions – try tiny corn muffins, spring rolls, nachos and potatoes. Snacks should be tasty and satisfying, although I cannot guarantee that you won't be back for more!

CONTENTS

MEXICAN CORN MUFFINS	86
NACHOS	86
GRILLED AUBERGINE SLICES	88
BRUSCHETTA	88
DEEP-FRIED POTATO & SPINACH 'SANDWICHES'	90
JACKET POTATOES	90
BABY CORNS WRAPPED IN BACON	92
SPRING ROLLS	92
STUFFED TOMATOES	94
STUFFED CABBAGE LEAVES	94

SNACKS

MEXICAN CORN MUFFINS

MAKES 18

Eat these tasty muffins warm, with butter if you like. They make ideal party food, if baked in mini tins, and they freeze very successfully.

175 g (6 oz) cornmeal
175 g (6 oz) plain flour, sifted
1 tablespoon baking powder
1 teaspoon salt
½ teaspoon bicarbonate of soda
½ teaspoon sugar
1 onion, chopped
2 red chillies, seeded and chopped
½ red pepper, cored, seeded and chopped
2 eggs, beaten
225 ml (8 fl oz) full-fat milk
125 ml (4 fl oz) vegetable oil
125 g (4 oz) Cheddar cheese, grated
198 g (7 oz) can sweetcorn, drained

1. Preheat oven to 200°C (400°F/Gas 6).

2. In a large bowl, mix together the cornmeal, flour, baking powder, salt, bicarbonate of soda and sugar.

3. Put the onion, chillies, pepper, eggs and milk in a food processor or blender, and work to a purée.

4. Add to the dry ingredients with the oil, cheese and sweetcorn. Stir until evenly blended.

5. Spoon into greased muffin tins and bake for about 20 minutes until risen and golden. Serve immediately.

NACHOS

SERVES 6

These disappear very quickly, so make lots! Vary the toppings, including ingredients such as canned salted black beans, sliced red onions and peppers. Try different cheeses too.

30 tortilla chips
298 g (10½ oz) can cream-style corn
1 avocado, diced
50 g (2 oz) Cheddar cheese, grated
2 red chillies, seeded and thinly sliced
pepper to taste
parsley sprigs to garnish

1. Preheat grill to high.

2. Arrange the tortilla chips in a single layer in a shallow ovenproof dish.

3. Put a heaped teaspoon of creamed corn on each one and top with the avocado. Sprinkle with the cheese and chilli slices and season with pepper.

4. Cook under the grill for 2-3 minutes until the cheese melts. Serve immediately, garnished with parsley.

ABOVE: MEXICAN CORN MUFFINS *BELOW*: NACHOS

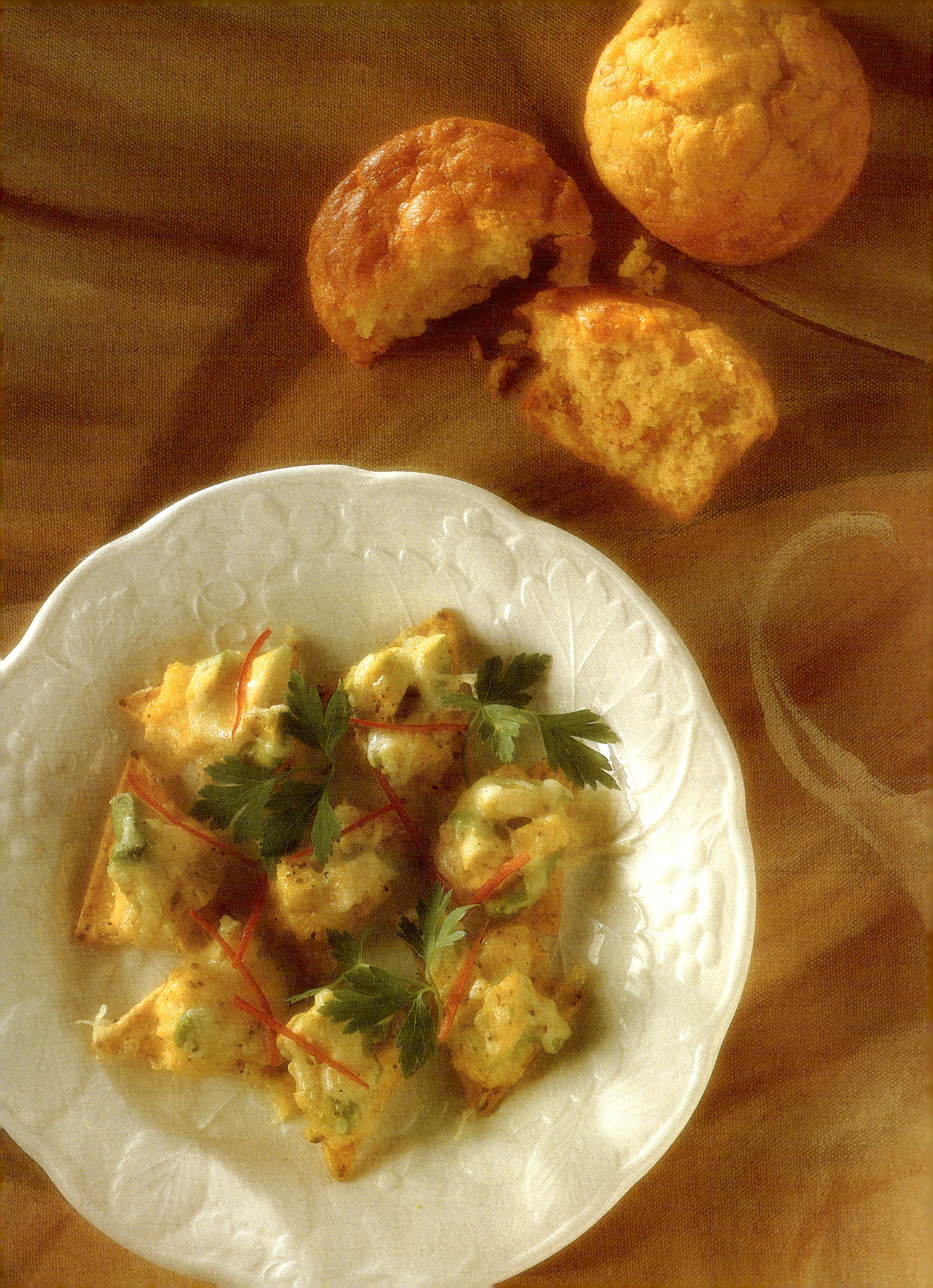

SNACKS

GRILLED AUBERGINE SLICES

SERVES 4

These are like mini pizzas – using large aubergine slices for the bases instead of dough. They make an excellent starter too.

1 large aubergine
olive oil for brushing
2×150 g (5 oz) mozzarella cheeses
8-12 tablespoons passata
pepper to taste
1 tablespoon chopped oregano
oregano sprigs to garnish

1. Preheat grill to medium and preheat oven to 200°C (400°F/Gas 6).

2. Cut the aubergine into 8-12 slices, each 1 cm (½ inch) thick. Brush both sides with olive oil. Grill for about 3 minutes on each side until golden.

3. Cut the mozzarella into as many slices as you have aubergine and place on top of the aubergine. Top each with a tablespoon of passata, a little olive oil and a sprinkling of pepper. Bake for about 5 minutes until the mozzarella has melted.

4. Sprinkle with the chopped oregano and serve warm, garnished with oregano sprigs.

BRUSCHETTA

SERVES 4

This Italian garlic bread calls for the best olive oil – preferably first pressed – for maximum flavour. Use plum tomatoes if possible.

4 ripe tomatoes
8 thick slices of crusty white bread
4 cloves garlic
6 tablespoons quality olive oil
salt and pepper to taste

TO GARNISH
torn basil leaves
olive slices

1. Preheat the grill to high.

2. Immerse the tomatoes in boiling water for 30 seconds, then drain and plunge into cold water. Carefully peel away the skins. Cut the tomatoes into quarters and discard the seeds. Chop roughly.

3. Toast the bread on both sides until golden brown. Rub one side of the hot toast with the cut garlic.

4. Place the toasts, garlic side up, on a serving dish and drizzle with the olive oil.

5. Pile the chopped tomato on to the toast and sprinkle with salt and pepper. Garnish with basil and olive slices. Serve immediately.

ABOVE: GRILLED AUBERGINE SLICES   *BELOW*: BRUSCHETTA

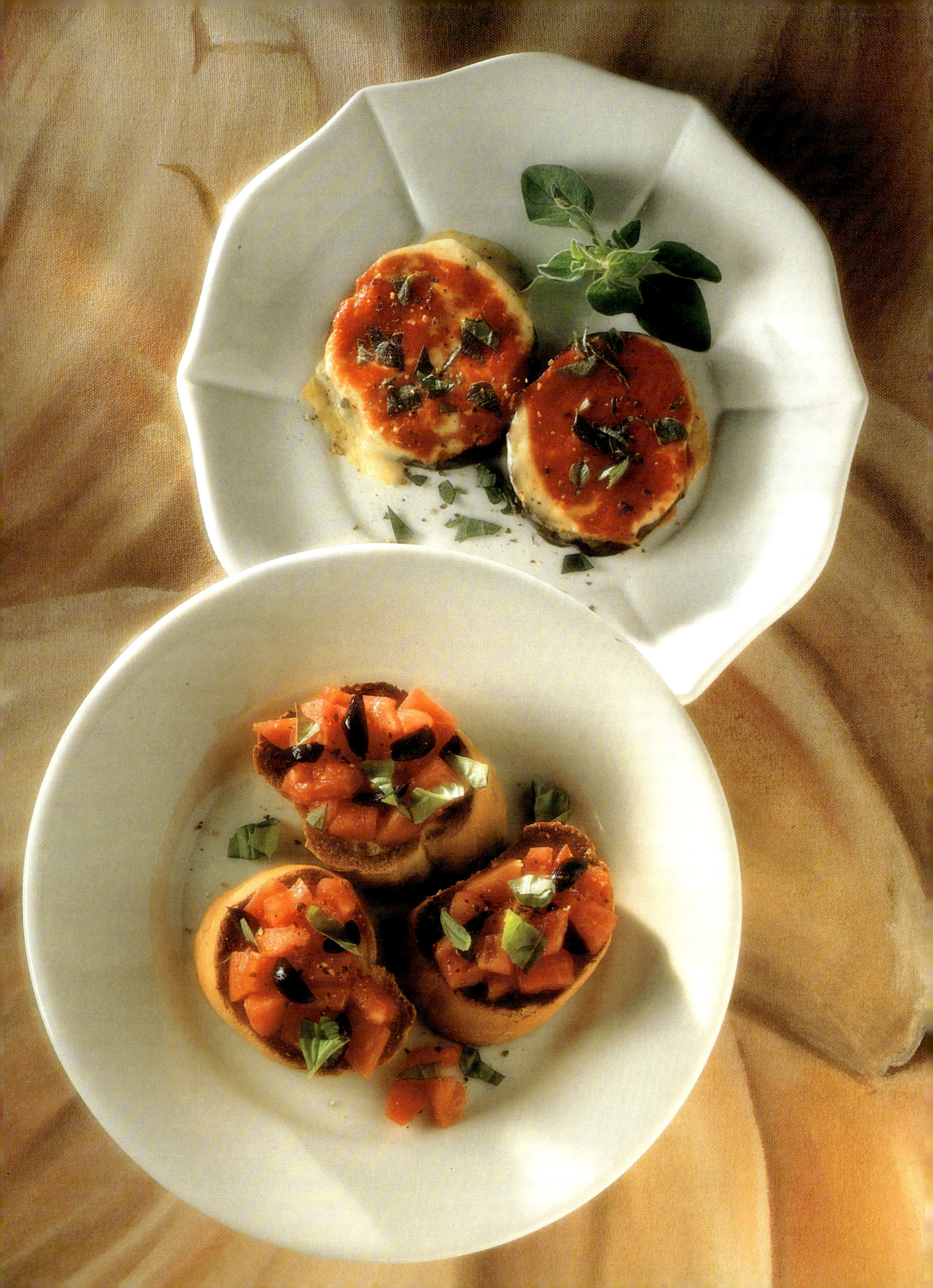

SNACKS

DEEP-FRIED POTATO & SPINACH 'SANDWICHES'

MAKES 8

These little snacks can be made in advance and reheated in the oven.

750 g (1½ lb) large potatoes
1 tablespoon olive oil
2 cloves garlic, crushed
250 g (8 oz) frozen chopped spinach
2 teaspoons black olive purée
salt and pepper to taste
50 g (2 oz) feta cheese, thinly sliced
1 egg, beaten
dry breadcrumbs for coating
vegetable oil for shallow-frying

1. Cut the potatoes into 1 cm (½ inch) slices; you need 16 good ones. Cook in boiling salted water for 5 minutes; drain.

2. Heat the olive oil in a pan, add the garlic and cook for a few seconds, then add the frozen spinach and cook until soft. Add the olive purée, season and cook, stirring, until all liquid has evaporated.

3. Spread the mixture evenly on half of the potato slices. Cover with cheese and top with remaining potato slices.

4. Pour oil into a deep frying pan to a depth of 2.5 cm (1 inch) and heat.

5. Brush the sandwiches with beaten egg, then coat evenly with breadcrumbs.

6. Shallow-fry for 4-5 minutes on each side, until golden brown. Drain on kitchen paper. Serve warm, with a tomato relish.

JACKET POTATOES

SERVES 4

Quick jacket potatoes filled with ricotta and sun-dried tomatoes, which are available from larger supermarkets and Italian delicatessens.

4 medium baking potatoes
125 g (4 oz) ricotta or curd cheese
4 large sun-dried tomatoes, chopped
1 tablespoon pine nuts
2 tablespoons chopped basil
1 tablespoon olive oil
salt and pepper to taste
extra olive oil

TO GARNISH
basil leaves
radicchio leaves

1. Cook the potatoes in the microwave, allowing 10-12 minutes on high per 500 g (1 lb), turning halfway through cooking. Alternatively, bake in a preheated oven at 220°C (425°F/Gas 7) for 1 hour, then lower temperature to 200°C (400°F/Gas 6).

2. Cut a slice off the top of each potato and scoop out the flesh, leaving a 5 mm (¼ inch) shell.

3. Mash three quarters of the potato flesh with the ricotta or curd cheese, sun-dried tomatoes, nuts, basil, oil and seasoning.

4. Fill the potatoes with the stuffing and microwave on high for 3 minutes or return to the oven for 10 minutes.

5. Drizzle with a little olive oil and serve garnished with basil and radicchio.

ABOVE: DEEP-FRIED POTATO & SPINACH 'SANDWICHES'   BELOW: JACKET POTATOES

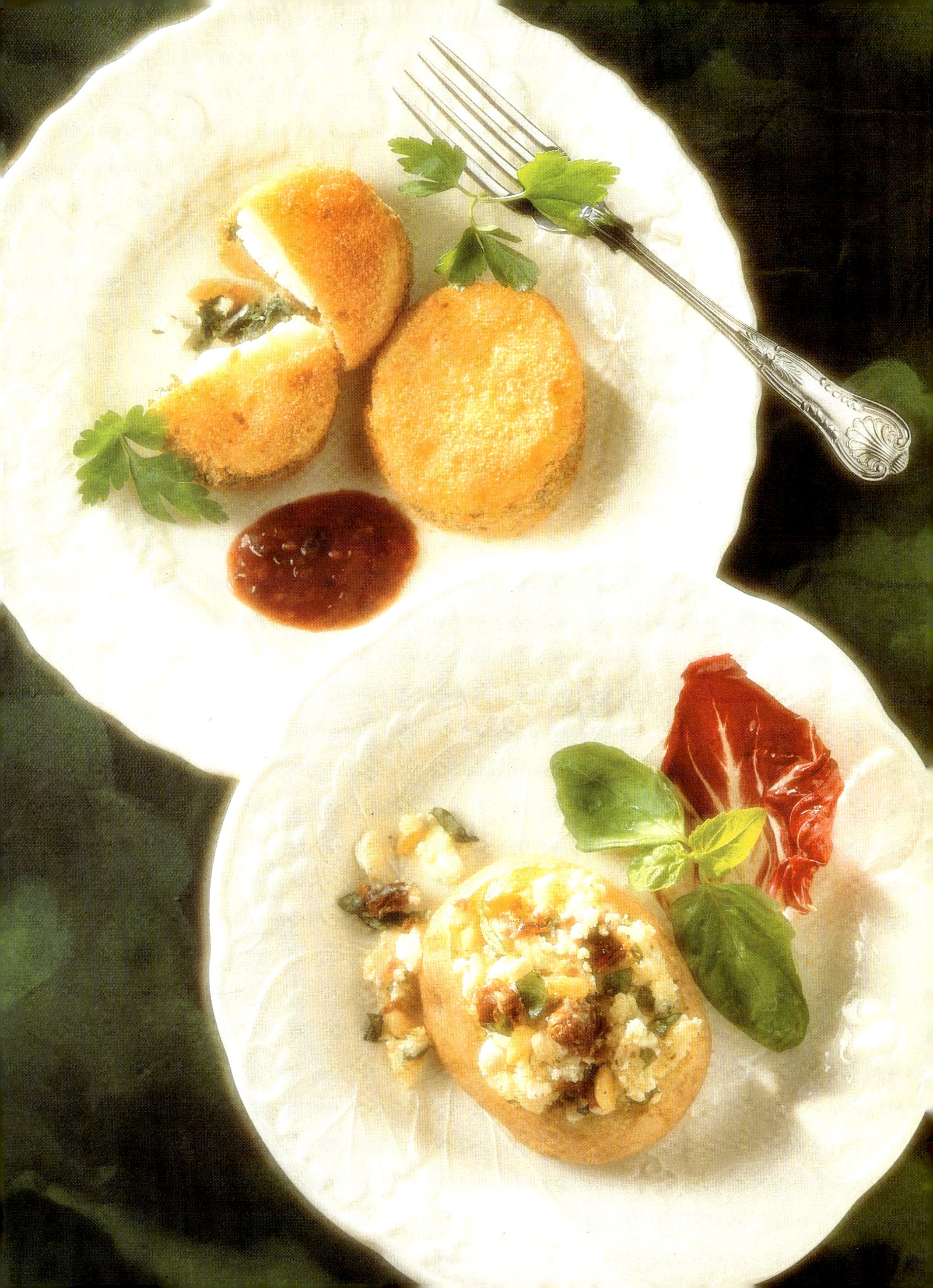

SNACKS

BABY CORNS WRAPPED IN BACON

MAKES 16

Another snack which works well as a party canapé – and equally successfully as a children's treat!

16 baby corn cobs
8 slices streaky bacon, derinded
olive oil for brushing

DIP
90 ml (3 fl oz) mayonnaise
1 tablespoon tomato ketchup
squeeze of lemon juice
few drops of Tabasco
salt and pepper to taste

TO GARNISH
parsley sprigs

1. Cook the baby corn in boiling salted water for 3-4 minutes. Plunge into cold water and drain. Dry on kitchen paper.

2. Preheat grill to medium. Halve each bacon rasher lengthwise and twist a strip around each corn cob, leaving the tip exposed.

3. Brush with a little oil and grill, turning, until the bacon is slightly crispy.

4. For the dip, mix together the mayonnaise, tomato ketchup, lemon juice, Tabasco and seasoning in a bowl.

5. Serve the corns warm, garnished with parsley and accompanied by the tomato dip.

SPRING ROLLS

MAKES 6

1 tablespoon vegetable oil
500 g (1 lb) frozen stir-fry mixed vegetables
1 teaspoon salt
1 teaspoon sugar
1 teaspoon light soy sauce
1 teaspoon dark soy sauce
1 teaspoon sesame oil
3 large sheets filo pastry, each about 42×30 cm (17×12 inches)
oil for brushing
coriander sprigs to garnish
chilli oil to serve

1. Preheat oven to 200°C (400°F/Gas 6).

2. Heat the oil in a wok or large frying pan. When very hot, add the vegetables and stir-fry for about 5 minutes. Drain off any excess liquid. Add the salt, sugar, soy sauces and sesame oil. Set aside.

3. Cut the filo sheets in half lengthwise to give 6 strips. Brush 1 strip lightly with oil and place 2 tablespoons of the stir-fried vegetables at one end, leaving a 5 cm (2 inch) border at the edge. Fold this over the vegetables and fold in 1 cm (½ inch) of the sides of the pastry. Roll up like a cigar and place on a lightly oiled baking sheet. Repeat with the remaining filo pastry and filling.

4. Brush the rolls lightly with oil and bake for about 20 minutes, until golden.

5. Garnish with coriander and serve with chilli oil for dipping.

ABOVE: BABY CORNS WRAPPED IN BACON *BELOW*: SPRING ROLLS

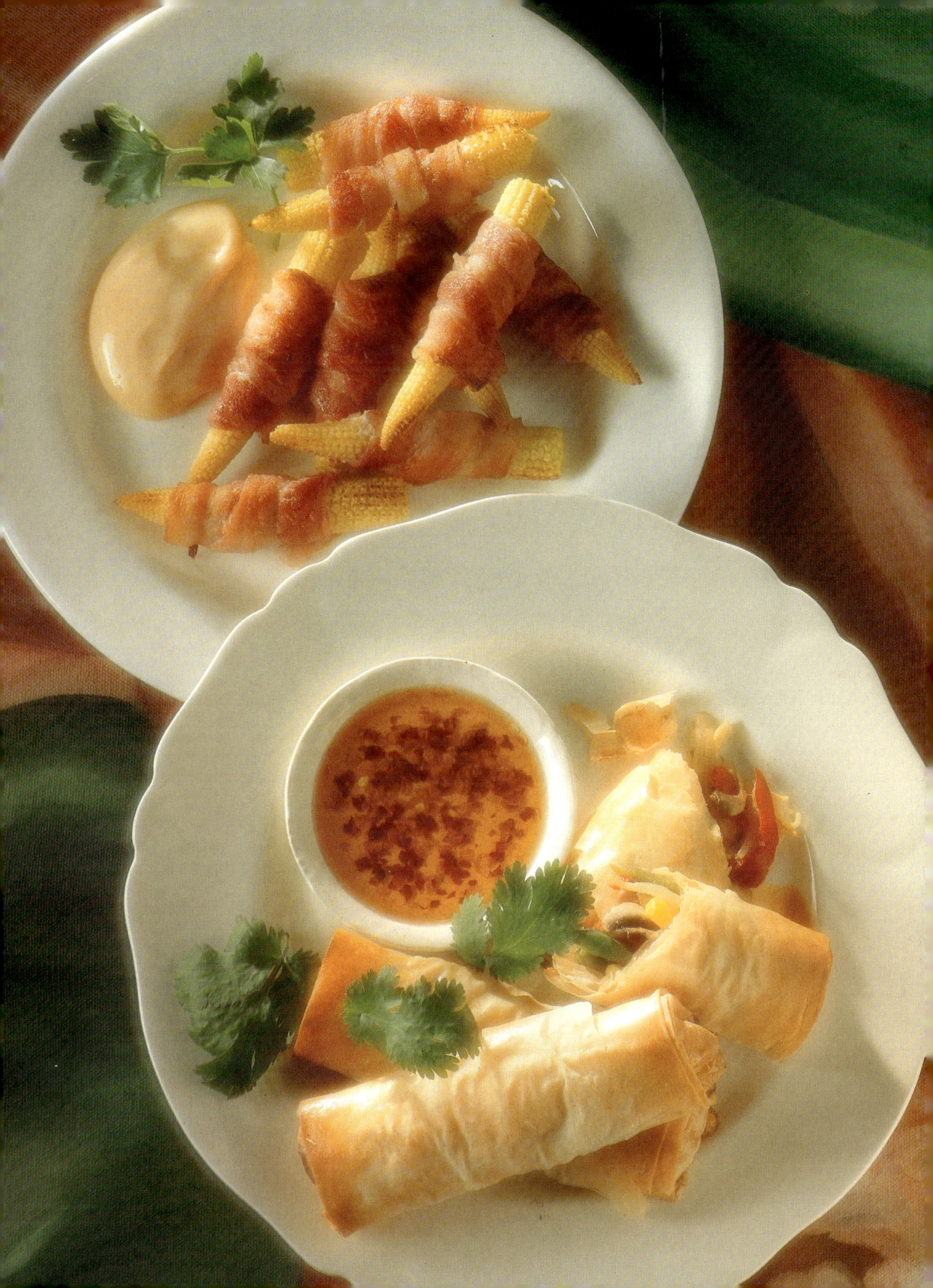

STUFFED TOMATOES

SERVES 4

For extra speed, cook these stuffed tomatoes in the microwave – on high for 3 minutes. Illustrated on back cover.

6 tablespoons bulghur wheat
4 beef tomatoes
salt and pepper to taste
50 g (2 oz) butter
1 onion, finely chopped
1 clove garlic, crushed
6 tablespoons chopped parsley
2 teaspoons chopped oregano
lemon wedges to serve

1. Put the bulghur wheat in a bowl, cover with water and leave to soak for 30 minutes.

2. Preheat oven to 200°C (400°F/Gas 6).

3. Meanwhile, cut the tops off the tomatoes and discard. Gently squeeze the tomatoes to remove the seeds and juice, leaving the fleshy parts in the tomato intact. Season.

4. Melt half of the butter in a pan, add the onion and cook until softened. Add the garlic and cook for 1 minute.

5. Drain the bulghur wheat and squeeze as dry as possible. Mix with the herbs, seasoning and sautéed onion and garlic.

6. Fill the tomatoes with the mixture and dot with the remaining butter. Place in a buttered ovenproof dish and bake for about 20 minutes until golden. Serve hot, accompanied by lemon wedges.

STUFFED CABBAGE LEAVES

SERVES 4

These are delicious served with warmed passata. Don't use cream cheese in place of curd cheese, as it melts when heated. Illustrated on back cover.

12 large cabbage leaves
25 g (1 oz) butter
1 small onion, chopped
8 rashers streaky bacon, derinded and chopped
125 g (4 oz) mushrooms, chopped
500 g (1 lb) curd cheese
½ teaspoon cumin
½ teaspoon thyme
salt and pepper to taste
1 egg, beaten
2 tablespoons oil

1. Blanch the cabbage leaves in boiling salted water for about 8 minutes, until tender. Drain, refresh in cold water and dry thoroughly on kitchen paper.

2. Melt the butter in a pan, add the onion and bacon and cook gently until the onion is soft. Add the mushrooms and cook for 1 minute. Add to the curd cheese with the cumin, thyme and seasoning; mix well. Beat in the egg.

3. Divide the mixture between the cabbage leaves. Roll up, tucking in the ends, to make parcels.

4. Heat the oil in a large frying pan. Add the cabbage parcels and fry gently for 15 minutes, turning once. Serve immediately.

INDEX

A
Artichoke with goat's cheese 12
Artichoke risotto 56
Asparagus in prosciutto 10
Aubergine:
 Grilled aubergine slices 88
 Marinated baby aubergines 10
 Pepper and aubergine pizza 48
Avocado:
 Guacamole 24

B
Bean:
 Broad beans with mushrooms and bacon 78
 Chilli bean and sausage casserole 60
 French bean bundles 74
 Tuscan bean soup 34
Beetroot:
 Baby beets with fromage frais 80
 Beetroot and fennel soup 36
Broad beans with mushrooms and bacon 78
Broccoli
 Pasta with broccoli and anchovies 52
 Stir-fried broccoli with hoisin sauce 70
Bruschetta 88

C
Cabbage:
 Stuffed cabbage leaves 94
Carrot:
 Carrot ribbons with mustard seeds 74
 Carrot roulade 14
 Sautéed carrot and courgette 68
Chard with garlic, stir-fried 66
Cherry tomato *see* Tomato
Chilli bean and sausage casserole 60

Corn:
 Baby corns with pepper salsa 8
 Baby corns wrapped in bacon 92
 Corn and pimiento fritters 82
 Mexican corn muffins 86
 Nachos 86
Courgette:
 Sautéed carrot and courgette 68
Couscous 50
Creole prawn gumbo 54
Crêpes:
 Spinach and ham crêpes 40
Crudités with pepper dip 20
Cucumber:
 Stir-fried spicy cucumber 70
Curried pumpkin soup 32

E
Egg:
 Carrot roulade 14
 Frittata 42
 Spinach and herb eggah 42

F
Fennel:
 Beetroot and fennel soup 36
French bean bundles 74
Frittata 42
Fritters:
 Corn and pimiento fritters 82

G
Gazpacho 36
Gnocchi with rocket sauce 44
Goat's cheese:
 Artichoke with goat's cheese 12
 Leek and goat's cheese tart 48
Gougère:
 Mushroom and chicken gougère 58
Gremolata 76
Guacamole 24

H
Hot and sour soup Thai-style 28

L
Leek and goat's cheese tart 48
Leek and pepper slice 14

M
Mexican corn muffins 86
Minted onion in toast cups 76
Mushroom:
 Broad beans with mushrooms and bacon 78
 Mushroom and chicken gougère 58
 Mushroom ragoût 16
 Stuffed mushrooms 12

N
Nachos 86
Noodle:
 Spicy glass noodle salad 22

O
Onion:
 Minted onion in toast cups 76
 Onion and gruyère jalousie 46
 Red onion and olive tartlets 18

P
Pasta with broccoli and anchovies 52
Pasta with ricotta, mushrooms and bacon 52
Pea and mint soup 32
Peas with radicchio 80
Pepper:
 Baby corns with pepper salsa 8
 Crudités with pepper dip 20
 Leek and pepper slice 14
 Pepper and aubergine pizza 48
 Sweet and sour pepper 'noodles' 68

Tomato and pimiento soup 30
Pistou vegetable soup 34
Pizza 48
Plantain:
  Sweet potato and plantain crisps 66
Pot-au-feu 60
Potato:
  Jacket potatoes 90
  Potato skins with herb dip 24
  Potato and spinach 'sandwiches' 90
Prawn:
  Creole prawn gumbo 54
  Prawn and mangetout stir-fry 56
Pumpkin:
  Curried pumpkin soup 32

R
Radicchio:
  Grilled radicchio and chicory 64
  Peas with radicchio 80
Radish:
  Glazed radishes 78
Ratatouille tartlets 18
Red onion and olive tartlets 18
Rocket:
  Gnocchi with rocket sauce 44
  Rocket soup with Parmesan 30

S
Soups 26-36:
  Beetroot and fennel soup 36
  Curried pumpkin soup 32
  Pea and mint soup 32
  Pistou vegetable soup 34
  Rocket soup with parmesan 30
  Thai-style hot and sour soup 28
  Tomato and pimiento soup 30
  Tuscan bean soup 34
  Watercress and lime soup 28
  White gazpacho 36
Spiced vegetables in poppadum cups 20

Spicy glass noodle salad 22
Spinach:
  Potato and spinach 'sandwiches' 90
  Spinach and ham crêpes 40
  Spinach and herb eggah 42
  Spinach rice pilaf 82
Spring rolls 92
Squash:
  Stuffed squash 44
Starters 6-24:
  Artichoke with goat's cheese 12
  Asparagus in prosciutto 10
  Baby corns with pepper salsa 8
  Carrot roulade 14
  Crudités with pepper dip 20
  Grilled vegetables with pesto 8
  Guacamole 24
  Leek and pepper slice 14
  Marinated baby aubergines 10
  Mushroom ragoût 16
  Potato skins with herb dip 24
  Ratatouille tartlets 18
  Red onion and olive tartlets 18
  Spiced vegetables in poppadum cups 20
  Spicy glass noodle salad 22
  Stuffed mushrooms 12
  Tomato soufflés 16
  Vegetable tempura 22
Stir-fried broccoli with hoisin sauce 70
Stir-fried chard with garlic 66
Stir-fried spicy cucumber 70
Stuffed cabbage leaves 94
Stuffed mushrooms 12
Stuffed squash 44
Stuffed tomatoes 94
Sugar snaps with coconut and chilli butter 72
Sweet potato and plantain crisps 66
Sweet and sour pepper 'noodles' 68
Sweetcorn *see* Corn

T
Tempura 22
Thai-style hot and sour soup 28
Tomato:
  Bruschetta 88
  Sautéed cherry tomatoes with herbs 72
  Stuffed tomatoes 94
  Tomato and pimiento soup 30
  Tomato soufflés 16
Tuscan bean soup 34

V
Vegetable:
  Baby vegetables with herb vinaigrette 64
  Grilled vegetables with pesto 8
  Pistou vegetable soup 34
  Roast vegetables with gremolata 76
  Spiced vegetables in poppadum cups 20
  Vegetable couscous 50
  Vegetable tempura 22
  Vinaigrette, herb 64

W
Watercress and lime soup 28